REFERENCE.

79. Sir G. Pauncefote Bar.t
80. Emmet Skidmore's
81. Skidmore's Wharf
82. The Park keeper's Lodge.
83. M.r Simeon Howard's
84. M.r Wild's.
85. Doctor Anderson's.
86. M.r Hemming's.
87. Geo: Cole Esq.r
88. M.r James's.
89. M.r Thomas Howard's.
90. John Swannel's.
91. Jennings's Mill.
92. Thomas Weedon's.
93. Eagleton's farm.
94. Wild's farm.
95. Sedgwick's farm.

REMARKS.

The Road from Amersham through Rickmersworth is part of the Cross road from Reading to Hatfield, 30 Miles.

‡ Mile stones

29 ‡
30 ‡
31 ‡ } Miles from Reading.
32 ‡
33 ‡
34 ‡

† Hand post, turn right to Chesham through Chenies, 6 miles. Left to Amersham 4½ miles

— At Chenies, the Monuments of the Bedford Family.

— A Stream rises at Chesham famous for Trout, Eels &c.n which meeting the Colne at Rickmersworth, flows onto the Thames at Brentford. It is marked in blue: It turns 8 Mills in its Course through this Map. Viz.t

1. Dodd's, for Paper & Flour.}
2. Stevens's — Paper
3. Meeke's — Paper
4. Jones's — Paper
5. Pindar's — Flour
6. Munn's — Paper
7. Strutt's — Cotton & Flour
8. Jennings's — Flour.

— The Grand Junction Canal passes near Rickmersworth, whereon are two Coal wharfs Viz.t

1. Skidmore's }
2. Salter's

From hence a considerable Trade is carried on, not only in Coal, but in Manure of various Sorts; in Timber, & other bulky Articles.

2. Through Batchworth to the right leads to Uxbridge; to the left to Moore Park; & strait on from the Cotton Mill up hill, to the new Enclosures towards Harrow.

The Valleys, Commons, Parks &c.a are light Green; the Woods darker; the rest is mostly arable Land. the Carriage roads are brown; the Lanes are single lines, the paths are dotted, & the Houses are red. The whole divided into Parishes by coloured Lines, & done from actual Measurement, by George Thomson. 1808.

adjacent, containing SIXTEEN square MILES.

The Book of Chorleywood & Chenies 1983
has been published in a Limited
Edition of which this is

Number 65

A complete list of the
original subscribers is printed
at the back of the book

THE BOOK OF
CHORLEYWOOD & CHENIES

FRONT COVER — ABOVE: The Old Chorleywood House, built by the Barnes
family; BELOW: The Manor House Chenies, 1932. (S)

The Chess, or Mousehawk Stream, coveted for its trout from Roman times.

THE BOOK OF CHORLEYWOOD & CHENIES

BY

GEORGE E RAY FDRCS

BARRACUDA BOOKS LIMITED
BUCKINGHAM, ENGLAND
MCMLXXXIII

PUBLISHED BY BARRACUDA BOOKS LIMITED
BUCKINGHAM, ENGLAND

AND PRINTED BY
BURGESS & SON (ABINGDON) LIMITED
ABINGDON, ENGLAND

BOUND BY
WOOLNOUGH BOOKBINDING
WELLINGBOROUGH, ENGLAND

JACKET PRINTED BY
CHENEY & SONS LIMITED,
BANBURY, ENGLAND.

LITHOGRAPHY BY
CHAPMAN BROTHERS LIMITED,
KIDLINGTON, OXFORD.

DISPLAY SET IN BASKERVILLE
AND TEXT SET IN 10½/12pt BASKERVILLE BY
KEY COMPOSITION, NORTHAMPTON, ENGLAND.

ISBN 0 86023 184 4

Contents

Foreword

by Lady A. L. T. Lewis

I was faintly surprised when Mr Ray asked me if I would write a foreword to his book on Chorleywood, and then I realised that, as I had spent half my somewhat long life here, and very happily too, perhaps it was not so unsuitable after all.

When we moved here in April 1933 I became involved in a branch of the National Council of Women, and involved — in one way or another — I have been ever since.

Mr Ray gives us a very clear picture of Chorleywood through the years; the war, the loss of independence and joining with 'Three Rivers' and the purchase of Chorleywood House — the subject of much heated discussion and which proved so very worthwhile.

I have found Chorleywood a very pleasant place in which to live and can heartily recommend it, and I am sure Mr Ray's book will help you to appreciate it.

Lorna Lewis

Acknowledgements

My thanks are due to so many that not all can be included, and I unreservedly apologise for any ommissions, but among those to whom I owe thanks a few must be mentioned. First, Lady Lewis, for writing the preface, then Clive Birch and Barracuda; Mrs Thomas for much of the detail on Chenies, Godfrey Cornwall to whom I owe the greatest of debts; Tom Darvell, Grelle White of the *Watford Observer*, Richard Darrah, the librarians of Chorleywood and Rickmansworth, Walter Hands, and the ladies of the Chorleywood Bookshop; the officers of the local authorities, Buckinghamshire Library Authority and their Amersham and Chesham branches for holding the essential subscription facilities, and Charlie Batchelor, Herbert Parsons, Ralph Gullett, Joyce Baker, and last but not least my wife, who has had to put up with the noise of my constant typing, and has kept me suitably fed and watered. To all of these and many more, my grateful thanks, and deep appreciation.

Introduction

It is almost impossible to go anywhere in Britain without being reminded of our ancient heritage, the legacy of the Romans, and the wealth of ancient monasteries, but even that encompasses only a brief period of the past which began with a civilisation as old as the Greek, and although less compact, greater than any Middle Eastern empire, even larger than the Roman. I speak of course of the Celts, who ruled for about 2,000 years before the Romans, and even in their time sacked Rome.

The Celts re-emerged after the Roman occupation, and it was the Celts of the Cilternsetae, who lived in and around Chorleywood and Chenies, using Verulamium as a base, who kept the Saxons at bay until late in the sixth century AD. Militarily the Chilterns controlled the Thames Basin, and its importance to London has been repeatedly exemplified in the history of these islands, during the Baronial War, the Wars of the Roses, the Civil War, and so on. It is therefore no accident which placed the massive Naval HQ at Northwood, the RAF at Halton, the Staff College at Latimer, or the Edwardian palace of Edward I and III at Kings Langley. Nor should it be surprising that in Callaghan's Cabinet, the bulk of his Privy Council were representatives of Celtic constituences. It is therefore entirely appropriate that the greatest living constituent, Lady Lewis, should have been the author of the foreword, and Welsh.

What makes the area unique is the fact that its two components, drawn from Herts and Bucks, belonged to chartered holdings, one secular and the other ecclesiastic. The contrasting evolution of the two is too large a subject for this brief work.

Even so the hints are there for the discerning to see, but that is not the object of the book which, reduced to its essentials, is and must be mainly a pictorial record of a place which has been and still is a place to love and cherish.

Dedication

This book is dedicated to the memory of two men: Geoffrey Cornwall, the founder of the Rickmansworth Historical Society, Gentleman, Miner, Singing Dustman, Clerk, and much else besides, without whose generosity this book could never have been written, and Robert Turney. Robert was an ex-policeman, a student of natural flora and fauna, an archetypal figure from the best and one of the oldest families of Chorleywood. May their memory never fade, humble by birth, but giants of men.

ABOVE: The Mill bridge, Chenies. The Mill lay to the north of the river, and west of the road; CENTRE: Soles Mill; BELOW: Loudwater Mill, home of *The Illustrated London News*.
(Note: Clive Birch, FSA FRSA, founder of Barracuda Books, was Director and Editor of *The Illustrated London News* 1969-1970 — Editor)

Uncommon Origins

Stone tools and part of the skull of an aurochs have been found locally. Stone Age man passed through, and the proximity to fertile ground of the ancient Icknield way, together with the finding of later flint tools, also indicates that Neolithic Man lived here. Certainly the Celts did, since we have archaeological evidence of two dwellings, one at Latimer and another at Chorleywood, of Belgic origin, both in similar juxtaposition to Roman villas, on the southern slopes of the valley. The villa remains were found first, and the Belgic sites later discovered, at Dell Farm by Brannigan, and at Loudwater by Sir Thomas Lewis and Howard Davies.

The Belgic remains in Chorleywood were somewhere in the pasture adjoining Chorleywood House, and are based on the accidental discovery of sherds found by the children of a Mr Rattle. On the advice of the then surveyor Walter Hands, they were taken to Verulamium for confirmation, but retained by the family, and on the order of the Council the site was covered to prevent desecration of the parkland.

The villa remains at Chorleywod are relatively sparse. They consist of part of a mosaic floor, which can now only be seen when the lily pond near Clearburn is emptied, a number of sherds, some roof tiles, and a coin of A.E. Valens, which suggest occupancy until the mid-fourth century. However, it enabled Sir Thomas and Mr Davies to estimate the size of the farm, a finding later confirmed by Brannigan.

Both villas were built after AD60 when the Iceni revolted, and probably date later, to the time when the Romans built a road between Verulamium and Silchester. A road was discovered by aerial survey by Margary in 1957, which lay along what is now North Hill, and passed across Phillipshill and on to Horn Hill. It would have been needed to convey building materials and produce to and from the villas.

The two villas lie at intervals of four Roman miles (a Roman mile being approximately nine tenths of an English mile). The first construction at Chenies consisted of a fairly simple dwelling, with a bath-house complete with mosaic floor at one end. As living standards improved, early in the third century four more rooms were added, together with a larger and more affluent bath house, and hypocaust heating under the south facing rooms. From then on, a number of further mosaics were added, until later in the century when, as a result of inflation, neglect and decay became evident, and the villa may even have become derelict. As the recession was alleviated and trade became more prosperous, the bath house was rebuilt, with even more complex mosaics, and a gatehouse and court-yard were added.

With the withdrawal of Roman forces to France, the state of the villa once more declined. There is also some indication that Britons continued to occupy it for a time after the Romans left. Curiously, while it is certain that the Saxons eventually came to live in the area, there is little archaeological evidence to support it. Moreover, we can assume, with a fair degree of confidence, that they did not do so until the middle of the sixth century, for at that time the name of

Rickmansworth was Rikmarsworp, the place of Rikmar, a sixth century British Queen of Essex. This coincides with the statement in the *Anglo-Saxon Chronicle*, which says that in AD560 Ceawlin gathered his forces in the forests of south-west Herts and Ashdown before marching on Aelle, near Southampton. In 571, he sent his chief lieutenant, Cuthwulf, back to take the towns of Limbury, Aylesbury, Benson, and Eynsham, and there is circumstantial evidence to support this in Chorleywood. For in 1977, while constructing an underground reservoir at Stag Lane, workers uncovered an earthenware pot full of Roman coins, while bulldozing the soil. These they tried unsuccessfully to sell, and they had to be recovered for the Water Company by the police.

The coins were examined by the British Museum and were found to be genuine. They are now kept at Rickmansworth, and a selection of them with the report of the Museum and a brief account of their finding has been beautifully mounted at their headquarters. Most of the coins pre-date AD330 and they were obviously used as common currency till a late date, but there is one of Theodora which, at the earliest, can only have been minted circa AD572 and the most obvious explanation is that some Briton hid them there and then was unable to reclaim them.

In later records of London, Rickmansworth and its environs is named as a hunting preserve for the wealthier citizens of that city.

The next specific mention of this area, in connection with the Saxons, dates to about the end of the eighth century, when Offa, the King of the Mercians, held a bridal party at the Moor in Rickmansworth. Here he is alleged to have murdered the groom, and in repentance is supposed to have moved to Holmesbury, where he is said to have founded the Monastery of St Albans.

This was the basis of the Liberty which included the manor of Prichemareswarde, and Chorleywood, as well as the main part of the Chess. He also gave at the same time 365 mancus to the Church of Rome for the maintenance of Peter's lights, a mancus being 30 pence, a gift which later the Pope tried unsuccessfully to make a fief, called Peters Pence.

Thereafter, there is little mention of either Rickmansworth or Chorleywood, except as they were part of the Liberty, until the time of William, and the Domesday record of 1086.

There is no record of either Chenies or Chorleywood in the Domesday Survey of 1986, but at that time Chorleywood was part of Rickmansworth which was recorded. In the Latin text it is called Prichmarewurde.

Sweeping almost due south-east through the valley at the foot of the Chilterns, the Chess flows through the village of Chenies and the town of Chorleywood, lying within the northern boundaries of both. There, it crosses the divide between Bucks and Herts, which also once divided the Honor of Wallingford from the Liberty of St Albans, both of which were lands held by ancient Charter.

An Honor consisted of a grouping of manors, knights' fees, or lordships, usually associated with a major castle. Before that, it consisted of thegndoms, which in this case were given by Queen Aelgiva to Edward the Confessor, and after the Conquest to Wigod, a thegn befriended by William, in return for passage at Wallingford over the Thames on his way to the Castle at Berkhamsted. Thereafter the castle and the Honor were given into the guardianship of William of Mortain, who lost it when he rebelled in 1104.

It then consisted mainly of holdings belonging to Richard D'Oyley, and Miles Crispin, along with parcels given to others, among whom was Manno, the Breton, who owned Isenhampstead (Chenies), and a larger holding, but not his chief demesne, at Chalfont St Giles.

Subsequently, most of the land passed with the Castle into the possession of the Prince of Wales, who retained it as overlord, though much of it was sold in free-hold, ie with the right of resale subject to the consent of the overlord.

The Liberty is slightly older, and was given with Albanestou Hundred to the Monastery of St Albans, (which dates to the same time), by King Offa c796, the grant being confirmed by Edward the Confessor, who appended his seal, and upheld its privileges, ie freedom from the Shire

Reeves' authority and normal taxes and tolls. It remained in Saxon hands after the Conquest, but, when the Abbot rebelled, it was confiscated, Kings Langley was alienated to the Honor and, at the request of Lanfranc, the Archbishop of Canterbury, was placed in the hands of Paul du Caen.

Chorleywood derives its name from Ceorla Leah, which means a clearing or meadow in the forest. In 1278, we know it had been changed to the Norman version, Bosco de Cherle (Peasant's Wood), and deeds of 1524 show it as Charleywoode. Thereafter it was known indiscriminately by phonetic interpretation as either Charleywood (the most common), or Chorleywood, which was finally decided on at the first meeting of the newly formed Urban District Council.

The main domicile in the Parish of Chenies was probably at Dell Farm, which was probably then known as the place on the river, but when Manno, the Breton, gave it for a knights' fee to Alexander de Isenhampstead, the probability is that he added the name of the place to his own, a custom still followed today. Isen, like Isel, or Isis, is a well known name for a river, a ham means a vill, and a stead or steading a place. Thus it probably means a vill at the place on the river. Alternatively Isen may be derived from the German Eisen meaning iron, but no iron workings of note have been found thereabout. Thence it passed, either by marriage or succession into the hands of the Cheyne family, whence it derived its present name of Chenies.

The Chess was probably called the Isen, but the first known name is the Pichelsburnae (the Mousehawk stream), which it was called in the records of St Albans at the time of the Peasant's Revolt. A later map shows it as the Lowdewater, another of 1805 the Chesham Stream, and today it has become known as the Chess.

It was an important river, the largest originally of the three, the Gade, the Chess, and the Colne, whence the name of Three Rivers was taken. It was a highly valued source of fishing, and power for a number of mills, one at Dell Farm, Latimer, one at Chenies, and two at Chorleywood. These mills were first used for grinding corn, later for cloth fulling, and even later for paper making.

In 1200 Chenies Mill was used solely for corn grinding, but by the 16th century it had been converted for cloth fulling. With the advent of print, and a popular press, the Dodds family of Sarratt bought it in 1740, and converted it into a paper mill. They retained it for about a century, until it became unprofitable, and was allowed to lapse.

The oldest of the mills at Chorleywood was Soles Mill, which expanded into print, when George Andrews bought it in 1746; he held it until 1756. It was then bought by Lewis Munn in 1817, (having in the interim had five previous owners), who constructed Solesbridge c1824, and sold it in turn to George Austin, whose descendants still live in the district.

When Austin took over the Mill it had four beating engines (though water was still the principal source of power), and it employed 35 workers: 18 men, 14 women, and 3 boys. The men worked a six day week of 12 hours a day (taking their meals at their work); the women worked from 8 am till 5 pm, and the boys earned 4 shillings a week, working practices which though harsh by modern standards, were regarded as humane for the time.

When it ceased to be profitable it was sold off, later becoming a trout and goldfish farm, and then the Highland Water Gardens.

Loudwater Mill has a similar history, was known to be in the possession of a Mr Jones in 1805, who sold it to Richard Weedon in 1816, who in turn sold it to Herbert Ingram.

Herbert Ingram was born in Boston, Lincs. in 1811, and was educated at the Boston Free School. At 14 he was apprenticed to Joseph Clarke, a printer of the Market Place, Boston. Then, in 1832, he joined with his half-brother, Nathaniel Cooke, in partnership as a journeyman printer, bookseller, and newsagent. In 1834, the firm of Ingram and Cooke bought off T. Roberts, a druggist of Manchester, an aperient pill. Ingram claimed he was given it by a descendant of *Old Parr* who, by taking this vegetable wonder drug regularly, was said to have survived to the wondrous age of 150, and in 1842, mainly to advertise the pill, the firm moved to London.

Meanwhile Ingram had projected an illustrated newspaper, *The Illustrated London News*, originally intended to be a weekly chronicle of crime. Henry Viztelly (who was employed on the paper) however, persuaded Ingram to give it a more general flavour. It published the Bow Street police reports, illustrating them with wood cuts by Crowquill, and by the use of the best artists and writers, steadily advanced its popularity, so that by 1852 it was selling a quarter of a million copies.

Meanwhile the partnership of Ingram and Cooke broke up, being dissolved in 1848, when Cooke retained the publishing business, and Ingram *The Illustrated London News*. In 1856 Ingram entered Parliament for Boston, at which time he had bought the Mill (1848), and was living at his new house, Glen Chess. He then made the mistake of allowing John Sadleir, a junior minister of the Treasury and MP for County Sligo, to associate his name with his brother (also Sadleir), in the issue of a number of fraudulent shares. In 1856, Sadleir committed suicide, and Vincent Scully took an action against Ingram to recover some of his losses. Ingram lost, but the Judge acquitted him of misconduct, leaving his honour unsullied.

Then in 1859, Ingram took his son on tour to America, chiefly to obtain illustrations for the Prince of Wales's tour. From there, he went to Canada, where he went on an excursion from Lake Superior to Lake Michigan. Unfortunately, the *Lady Elgin*, on which he travelled, collided with another, and on 8 September 1860, all on board were drowned.

The mill was then bought by William McMurray, a staunch Methodist, who left it to his nephew McFarlane, since when Glen Chess was turned into flats, and the mill and coach house into private residences.

The 1777 map of Andrews and Dury shows three Greens or Commons in the district, one at the Swill, whence the Swillett, which has been entirely enclosed, two Greens at Chenies one of which has been enclosed, and the Common at Chorleywood. A swill was a deep bowl formed within gravel; the Swillett has never been known to run dry and now overflows into a drain in Quickley Lane.

The northern part of the Common also lies on a gravel bed, the gravel having been brought down during the post-Ice Age melts, and is known to lie in places up to 100 feet in depth. But the southern half is chalk and flint, materials indigenous to the area, originally forming part of the sea-bed, and originating from the fossilised remnants of sea-creatures, some of which can still be found in local gardens. Changes in the sub-soil are reflected in the flora of the Common, that in the north such as bramble, liking acid soil, and those of the south, such as vetches, liking an alkaline environment.

There were two sets of Enclosure Acts, one preventing enclosure, the other permitting them in the interests of more intensive farming. But much depended on local feeling and the discretion of landlords. In Chorleywood and Chenies good sense prevailed, and the Green of Chenies, and the Common of Chorleywood were kept. A document photographed by kind permission of the Darvell family, shows the details of the conveyance of a parcel of the Common to George W. Wilson for an annual payment of 3s 6d.

Between then and the purchase of John Barnes in 1822, the agreement must have lapsed, because in 1819 a second agreement between John Barnes and John Dawes, and the Lord and copyold tenants was drawn up whereby a similar piece of land (in extent one acre and 30 perches) was exchanged for an equivalent piece of Oakfield and Little Ease.

A photostat of the original document was held by Robert F. Turney of the Retreat, and another copy, held by Henry Ryman, is now in one of the scrapbooks kept at the Chorleywood library, but there is some doubt as to the siting of the land given in exchange. In all probability it was land to the south-east of Sunshine House, then inhabited by Mr Barnes, and another small section of the land now forming part of the Common, immediately in front of Chorleywood House. In 1824, a further small piece was also exchanged to the Chorleywood House estate for a piece of Colliers. Presumably, this was part of Collyers field, now known as Colleyland, and originally part of the Berkhamsted poor estate, adjoining Hole Farm.

Both titles are attested and signed by the names of the numerous commoners (copyhold tenants) who possessed rights of common usage, conveyed with titles of property 'from time immemorial'. Unfortunately, these properties are not listed, but their location can be surmised from the list of Commoners of 1968, when by law the rights of the Common were invested in the District Council. These were George Harry Darvell of the Paddock, Jesse Wright Darvell of Crindau, Robert Ferrabee Turney of the Retreat, Phillip William Thomas Kime, Clements Farm, and Eric William Rambaut Fairley of Shepherds Cottage. The first two lay at the side of the Common near the Dell where the Arklow kennels were, the third lay in Chorleywood Bottom opposite the protected Tudor Cottage owned by Mrs Holliday, the fourth was situated on the corner of Clements Road, and the last was the pretty small cottage next door to the Shepherds Inn on the corner of the Common, as one emerges from the Bottom.

The regulation of the Common is described by another document of 2 August 1839, when a meeting of the Commoners was called at the Gate Inn, and sheds an interesting light on the then state of affairs. Several resolutions were passed: 1. that rights on the Common be invested exclusively in occupiers of land within Chorleywood; 2. that the cottagers who now turn sheep out on to the Common should be barred from couchancy or levancy, ie permanent pasture on the Common, and be given notice not to trespass in future; 3. that owing to its size, the number of sheep and lambs allowed to graze there be restricted to 1,000.

Several other resolutions were also carried, mainly having to do with details of the former, which resulted from the close cropping of sheep, which adversely affected the grazing of other animals. The copy deed was placed in the custody of Robert Turney, carrying the names of other commoners who were then, John Barnes, Lewis Munn, William Belch, W. White, W. Dorrofield, W. Watson, George Gardner, Daniel Swain, Job Johnson, Isaac Lovett, John Abbee, Abraham Farnborough, George Thomson, James Coster, William Briggs, Samuel Putnam, James Abbee, and John Pratt.

At this time the Common was largely covered with gorse, whose yellow bloom made a perfect picture; there were almost no trees, and the grazing rights were still an essential and considerable part of the local economy. However, the increasing use of the Common began to have a serious effect on the pasturage of animals, and this in turn led to many bitter disputes. While it was solely used for walks, children's games, hunting, riding, and the occasional game of cricket, football, or quoits, little difficulty arose. But when first the Cricket Club, then the Golf Club, and finally the Football Club, were instituted, these sports seriously interferred with grazing, and by 1910 Mr Gilliat was heartily sick of it. He therefore instructed his steward, Mr Atkins, to use the good offices of Mr Darvell to obtain some general agreement and, following another meeting of the Commoners, an agreement to restrict grazing was reached, and a nominal state of peace achieved. One or two souls still held out and made an occasional nuisance of themselves, but for practical purposes, a Pax Charleywood was achieved.

Mr Gilliat was then Lord of the Manor, and as such had the right of mining the Common. When, therefore, the railway was extended in 1888 from Rickmansworth to Chesham, a considerable number of navvies arrived in the area. Most settled in Rickmansworth and Mill End, but some found accommodation in Chorleywood, and proved an embarassment, some 40 huts being erected to house the men and their families. After the work was finished with gravel dug from the Cedars in the vicinity of the Black Horse, these men acquired squatters' rights, and within the workings a series of more permanent houses was built to accommodate them, and some encroachment on to the Common could no longer be avoided. This was further exacerbated by the objection of Mrs Gilliat to the presence of a public house on her land at Constables Cottage, then Finch's Arms. To solve the problem, Gilliat bought the small steading which was once believed to have belonged to some charcoal burners, and transferred the 'obnoxious' nuisance of the pub to its present site, when it was renamed the Black Horse.

Finally, with the advent of the motor car, the problem of parking arose. By this time, the regulation of the Common had passed to the Council, who inherited it from Henly Batty by deed of gift in the early 1920s. Batty wanted in fact to pass the whole Manor to the Council, but as it had for practical purposes no financial value, and included a covenant for the upkeep of Batchworth Bridge, they were reluctant to accept, though anxious to obtain the Common. Batty was agreeable and, after some negotiation, the Manor passed to Rickmansworth, and the Common to Chorleywood. Parking has proved a problem ever since and is strictly regulated, but the motor car had come to stay and some provision had to be made. In most parts it has been strictly circumvented by embankment, and the position has been regulated following the Act of 1968, when the rights of the Commoners were finally alienated, and the total responsibility conveyed legally to the local authority.

ABOVE LEFT: Aurochs' horn found at Tolpotts when making up Tolpitts Lane for Wolsley; (GC) RIGHT: primitive Paleolithic flint tool; (GC) BELOW LEFT: a more advanced form of flint Paleolith; (GC) RIGHT: Paleolithic hand-axe probably used for extracting bone-marrow. (GC)

ABOVE LEFT: Neolithic oyster flake; (GC) RIGHT: the Hollybush Pond, between the first and ninth fairways, thought to be Neolithic; CENTRE: Bronze Celt; (GC) and BELOW: a three cwt fragment of Sarsen stone; part of a block weighing several tons, found when making up Shire Lane, and now outside the Hurstleigh Home for the Elderly.

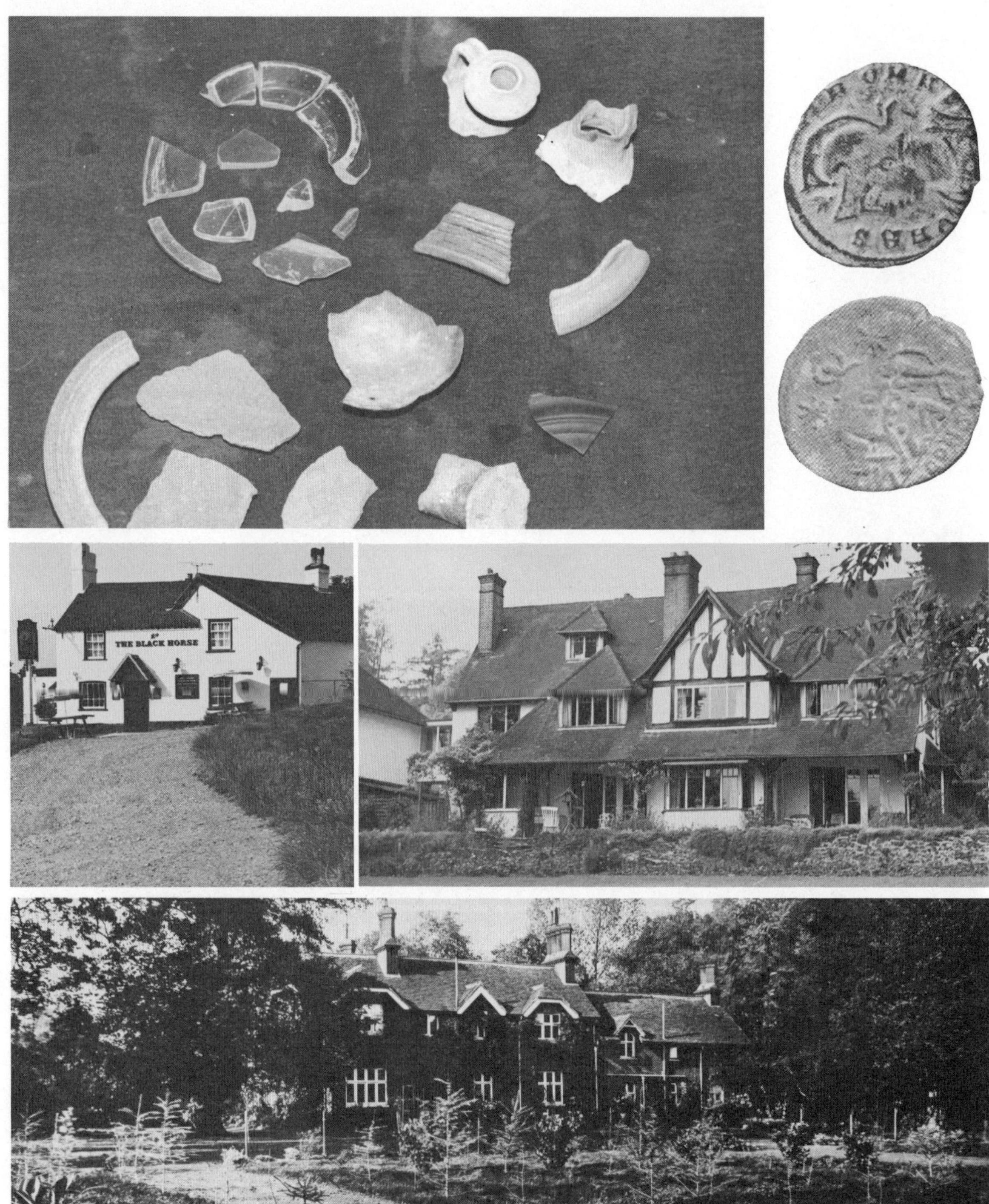

ABOVE LEFT: Sherds found at the Chorleywood Villa site: top left, Samian ware; RIGHT: Roman coin, minted at Rome; found near Stag Lane; CENTRE LEFT: the Black Horse, originally the site of a charcoal burner; RIGHT: Clearburn, the home of Lady Lorna, and Sir Thomas Lewis (the eminent cardiologist). The Chorleywood Villa is covered in to the south of the river in these grounds; BELOW: Dell Farm, Latimer, built to the east of the covered villa site. (S)

ABOVE: Common looking towards the cricket ground and Church, the bracken and heather indicating the acid subsoil; BELOW: the more open Common further south, as the soil changes from gravel to chalk; INSET: Glen Chess, built for Herbert Ingram, later known as McFarlanes.

ABOVE: The Manor House, Chenies, 1812; (MM) BELOW: the Royal Oak Chenies, 1906, believed to commemorate Elizabeth I's visit to Chenies but possibly older.

Lords of the Land

Alexander de Isenhampstead acquired the Manor of Chenies in 1165, and is thought to have been a direct ancestor of Alexander Cheyne, who held the gift of advowson to the Church there in 1232.

In extent, it was bordered by the river to the north, the Liberty to the east, by Chesham to the west, and by the Chalfonts to the south: roughly 3,000 acres in area.

Alexander Cheyne died in 1247, and his son John then became Sheriff of Beds and Bucks, but ran into debt. In order to repay that, he sold off some land, and mortgaged the rest to the King, who allowed his widow a small pension. John was succeeded by Bartholomew in 1296, and by his grandson Alexander in 1346 who, with his wife, Margaret, held the Manor once again free of debt. The next John Cheyne (1350) was made Sheriff of Beds and Bucks in 1371, and a Knight of the Shire in 1373. He was also a Gentleman of the Bed Chanber, and a Lollard, for which he was condemned to death, though the sentence was commuted by the House of Lords to life imprisonment.

The next heir was also John, whose wife Agnes brought him Cogenhoe Manor as part of her dower. He was returned to Parliament in 1413 and 1430, and after Agnes's death he married Isabel Mortimer. Thereafter, the Manor passed through several hands, by agreement with his son Alexander, via a trustee to Thomas Cheyne, then to Sir John Cheyne, both of Chesham,. the last Sir John dying without issue; thence via his wife Agnes to her second husband Edmund Molyneux, and by deed back to her niece Anne, and by entail to her son by her first husband Hugh Sapcote, through their son Guy to his daughter Anne.

Anne Sapcote married Sir John Broughton, who predeceased her, leaving her Thornaugh as well as Chenies, after which she married Sir Richard Jerningham and, outliving them both, finally married Sir John Russell. Russell belonged to the Dorset branch of the family of Hugo de Rosel who settled near Berwick. Under Henry VIII, he rendered stalwart service and was knighted on the field at Morlaix, where he lost an eye. Subsequently, he was ordered to convey the shipwrecked Archduke and his Duchess to the Manor of the Moor where he came once again to the notice of Henry, who made him his steward of the Moor, then after Russell's recommendation of Thomas Cromwell, his Lord Privy Seal, creating him an Earl in 1549. In the early '50s, however, he contracted a fatal fever, throughout which he was devotedly nursed at Chenies, though it was at his house near Westminster in 1554 that he finally died. He was granted a state funeral which took him to his final rest at Chenies. The Earldom passed to his son Francis, who had been educated at King's Hall, Cambridge, where he came under Protestant influence and was imprisoned by Mary for refusing to adopt Catholicism. His release, after petition, took him abroad, but he returned as soon as Elizabeth came to the throne and was favoured with his father's former office of Lord Privy Seal, and the gift of the Manor of the Moor.

In July 1557 Elizabeth visited Chenies, celebrating the occasion by planting an oak. She remained there from 19 July till 13 August, and held several meetings of her Privy Council.

Francis's sons predeceased him, and the title and inheritance passed to his grandson Edward, who was then a boy of 13. Edward was foolish enough to be influenced by Essex, whose early exploits had made him something of a hero, but then Essex insulted Elizabeth and after further indiscretions was executed for treason. Edward married the daughter of John Harrington. She was later made lady-in-waiting to Anne, the wife of James I and, when he died, the estate passed to his cousin Francis, who is renowned for draining the Fens, to what became known as the Bedford level. The fifth Earl William, the eldest son of Francis, sided with the Parliamentarians but, after Edgehill, transferred his allegiance to Charles, when he fought at the first Battle of Newbury. In so doing, he showed again the strain between loyalty and conscience which seems to have constantly bedevilled this renowned and talented family. Thereafter, he remained steadfast, and for his part in the restoration of Charles II he was created Duke in 1694.

His eldest son never married, died without issue, and Francis's second son, William, Lord Russell, carried the Bill of Exclusion in the Lords in 1680, after which he was involved with Monmouth, Charles II's eldest natural son, in his abortive Rye House Plot, for which he was executed. William had married Rachel Wriothesley, and his son, named after his mother's family, became second Duke. Possibly because of his disenchantment with the Parliamentary cause, and the close affiliation of Chenies, Chorleywood, and the neighbourhood with resistance to Charles, he moved the family home to Woburn, but their bodies have been returned one by one to the family vault at Chenies, where they lie in their velvet covered coffins, surmounted either by coronet or sword. Despite their change of domicile, the Manor remained in the family, until well into the twentieth century.

Chorleywood was part of the Manor of Rickmansworth, the major and older of the two market towns of the Soke, of which the second was Watford. As an adminstrative manor it came under the Soke, but parcels were sold off by subsequent Abbots from the time that it came into the possession of Paul du Caen after the rebellion of Fritheric. Each went to a major landowner or person of substance, and acquired manorial title.

After the Dissolution it passed out of the hands of the Liberty, which ceased to exist, to the Bishopric of London. However, it was reclaimed for the Crown by Elizabeth, though it still remained within the See, to provide funds for the Treasury. In Cromwell's day it was owned by John Fotherly, who played a part in the restitution of the Monarchy, and left it to his nephew Henry, conditional on his taking his name. Henry lived in great style and impoverished the estate, building a new Manor House in the Park and, when he died, his wife Mary married his solicitor, Thomas Deaton. They squandered the rest, ending in a debtors' prison. When, by order of the Court in Chancery, the Park with its Mansion was sold to Mrs Temperance Arden, the Manor went to Robert Williams of Moor Park.

Thereafter it passed by sale into various hands, until it was bought by John Saunders Gilliat, who built his new Manor House at the Cedars in Chorleywood. Thenceforth, until the end of the feudal system it remained in Chorleywood. The last lord after John Gilliat's son, Babington Gilliat, was Henly Batty, who wished to give it to Chorleywood. However, since this entailed the upkeep of Batchworth Bridge, the Council were unwilling to accept it. Henley therefore divided, it passing thte Common to the Council and the rest of the manorial rights back to Rickmansworth.

OPPOSITE ABOVE: Manor House Chenies, c1930; and CENTRE: in 1983;
LEFT: old remains of Manor, 1983, and RIGHT: Bury Park, Rickmansworth
Manor House, built for Henry Fotherly Whitfield.

It is difficult to state the exact annual income derived from the Copyholds now held of this Manor; the Fines, however, are arbitrary, and the Heriots the best beast,—failing that, the best chattel.

The Manor lies mixed with, or adjoining or near, the estates of the Earl of Essex, Lord Ebury, and other aristocratic proprietors.

The Neighbourhood is considered to be as select as any in the Kingdom.

The Quit and Free Rents amount to about £18 per annum; Rent of Market House, £3. 9s.; Tolls, £1 per annum.

The annual value of the Copyhold Estates has been carefully estimated, the manumission of which, with Heriots, &c., it is considered would amount to a considerable sum. Particulars of such estates are in the hands of the Auctioneer.

There are also Five Almshouses, paying no rent, of which the Lord has the right of nomination.

The Manor is liable, jointly with certain demesne lands, to the repairs of Batchworth Bridge, and the Market House is subject to an annual payment of £5; being part of an annual payment of £10 towards the support of the Almspeople in the five Almshouses.

The purchaser of the Manor will be at liberty to appoint his own Steward.

CONDITIONS OF SALE.

I. The highest bidder shall be the purchaser, and if any dispute shall arise between two or more bidders, the same shall be put up again at a former bidding.

II. No person shall advance a less sum at any bidding than shall be specified by the Auctioneer at the auction, and no person shall retract any bidding.

III. The purchaser shall, immediately after the sale, pay a deposit of £20 per cent. on the amount of his purchase-money to the Auctioneer, and sign an agreement for payment of the remainder of his purchase-money on the 16th day of July now next, at the office of Messrs. DAVIDSON, BRADBURY, and HARDWICK, Weavers' Hall, Basinghall-street, London, the vendor's solicitors, at which time and place the purchase is to be completed.

IV. Within seven days after the signing of the agreement for purchase, the vendor shall, at his own expense, deliver to the purchaser a copy of the abstract of title which was delivered to him on his purchase from a former owner. The vendor will also deliver to the purchaser an abstract of the conveyance to himself, and of a subsequent deed hereinafter referred to. The title of the vendor to the manor having been recently passed for purpose of enfranchisement by the copyhold commissioners, the fact of their passing or approving such title shall be deemed sufficient evidence of title down to that time; and for saving useless trouble or expense, the vendor expressly stipulates that no objection or requisition of any kind shall be made thereon; and the vendor will produce, with the title deeds, the commissioners' certificate, passing or approving his title, as above mentioned. The purchaser shall, on the settlement of the purchase, and on any title deeds or documents being handed over to him, execute to the

LEFT: Parsonage Farm, given by Elizabeth I to the Bishop of London in exchange for Rickmansworth Manor; RIGHT: Moor Park from the Temple Gardens — Rickmansworth Manor House in the time of Robt Williams; in the Wardenship of Sir John Russell; BELOW: sale notice of the Manor in 1925.

RICKMANSWORTH.

PARTICULARS

OF THE

VALUABLE

MANOR OF RICKMANSWORTH,

IN THE

COUNTY OF HERTS,

TOGETHER WITH

A COURT LEET, COURT BARON,

Quit Rents, Fines, Heriots, Rights, Royalties, &c.,

MARKET HOUSE, MARKET GROUND, STALLAGE, AND PROFITS AND TOLLS OF MARKET,

With the RIGHT of NOMINATING the OCCUPIERS of FIVE ALMSHOUSES in RICKMANSWORTH.

ALSO,

The Lord's Interest in an Extensive and Valuable Common,

CALLED

CHORLEY WOOD COMMON,

A Plan of which is hereto annexed,

CONTAINING ABOUT TWO HUNDRED ACRES;

Which will be Sold by Auction, by

MR. MARSH

AT

THE MART, OPPOSITE THE BANK OF ENGLAND,

ON

THURSDAY, THE SEVENTH DAY OF JUNE, 1860,

AT TWELVE O'CLOCK,

(UNLESS PREVIOUSLY DISPOSED OF BY PRIVATE TREATY.)

Particulars may be had of Messrs. DAVIDSON, BRADBURY, and HARDWICK, Solicitors, Weavers' Hall, Basinghall-street, City; at the MART; and of Mr. MARSH, at his Offices, 2, Charlotte-row, Mansion House.

LEFT: Sale notice of the Manor in 1825; ABOVE: the Cedars, built for John Gilliat MP, who bought the Manor from Williams, and BELOW: the Manor House Chorleywood, the last Manor House of Rickmansworth, and the home of the last owner, Henly Batty.

ABOVE: Loudwater House from the river early 20th century, (HCC) and CENTRE: the entrance, 1983; LEFT: the Coach House, 1983, and RIGHT: Clements Farm.

Of High Estate

The first part of the Park sale ordered by the Court in Chancery, was closely bound up with land at Loudwater, and was left by Mrs Arden to her son Joseph, who rebuilt the mansion which now houses the Masonic school for girls. At that time he bought the adjoining property of Loudwater. This is shown in Andrews and Dury's 1777 map, as mainly farm land with a few large copses, and an orchard, with mill cottages at either end. It was bounded to the north by Sarratt Lane, to the west by Solesbridge Lane, to the south by the turnpike, and at the east, by Loudwater Lane, with the probable exception of Glen Chess, an anomalous parcel to the west of Loudwater lane which Ingram later insisted should remain within the parish of Rickmansworth.

When Joseph Arden bought it, it was held in trust as part of James Hayward's estate, in the occupancy of Joseph Samuda. At that time the land was described as consisting of a large mansion, a farm, wood, park and farm land. James must have acquired it c1815-1820, for the mansion, now converted into flats, was originally built about then. Both the architecture, and spores found in some rot definitely identified as of French origin, suggest a date of 1820, when it is almost certain that prisoners of the Napoleonic wars were used in its construction.

The first definitive record is in the census of 1841, which shows it in the occupancy of James Hayward and his family. James seems to have been a wealthy man of singular distinction. He was a prime mover in the creation of Chorleywood parish, and held its first advowson, dying in the last months of the Crimean War at the early age of 48. By that time, however, the family had left the area, and Mrs Arden donated a tablet to the new Church, to commemorate both her husband and his eldest son Charles Augustus. This tablet is undoubtedly inaccurate, for it only mentions Charles, to whom it ascribes the winning of the Crimean medal with two clasps, the Croix de Légion de Honneur, the Sardinian medal, and the Turkish medal of Medijie, which it says he won during action with the naval brigade during the war. However, it also adds that he died as a midshipman serving aboard HMS *Virago* in 1858, which would have made him 16 at the time these decorations were won. To say the least, it is unlikely that a young midshipman could have won not only the long service campaign medals, but such elevated distinctions in one action at that date. The most likely explanation is that both father and son served in that war, and that it was the father who received them. This error is entirely credible, for her letter and gift were given by the widow, after her son died off Montevideo of yellow fever, when she was living at Cheltenham.

According to *Kelly's Directory*, the mansion then passed into the occupancy of Richard Baxendale in 1855, and in 1867 it was let to Viscount Malden, after which it was rented by Joseph Samuda, who remained there till his death, and who held it at the time of the sale in 1868.

Joseph Samuda, 1813-1885, was the second son of Abraham Samuda, a stockbroker and East and West India merchant, who trained in engineering under his elder brother Jacob. In 1832, the two went into partnership to construct marine engines. For a time he was also concerned with the development of the Atmospheric Railway, and then from 1843, he went into the construction of naval and merchant ships. Together with Edward Reed, he was a founder of the Institute of Naval

Architects, and from 1860-1865 sat on the Board of the Metropolitan Railway, which he left on being returned for Tavistock in the Liberal interest. In 1868, he was returned again, this time for Tower Hamlets, and served as a Captain with the Tower Hamlets' Rifle Volunteers, before being promoted to the rank of Lt Colonel.

Joseph Arden died in 1879, leaving his estate to his wife, with the exception of Loudwater, which he left in trust to his daughter, and her husband John William Birch, for their son Henry William. However, the two estates were not long separated, for Mrs Arden subsequently sold the Bury to John, who was then a Governor of the Bank England, a position later also held by his son Henry who, on marrying widow Mrs Hazeltine Conger, endowed her with an annual sum of £200, from the rents of Loudwater. Henry then went bankrupt, after which the couple resided at the Lodge, near Troutstream Way.

The estate was then bought by Cameron Jeffs, who with the help of his in-laws, the Darvell family, developed the estate, selling the large house to Wing Commander Frederick George Garrod, who in turn sold it to an architect, Gordon Symondson, who carried out the conversion and made many repairs, adding a charming modern villa, Chess Bord, within its grounds.

Apart from James Hayward, and Joseph Samuda, the most colourful character to have occupied it was Panmure Gordon, who rented it from Henry William Birch.

According to the documents of sale in 1825, what was for sale were the quit rents, fines, heriots, rights royalties etc, of the Market House, and the stallage, profits and tolls of the market and in addition, the lord's interest in the extensive and valuable Common at Chorleywood, containing about 200 acres. The exact income from copyhold was arbitrary, depending on the value of the property and the number of conveyances, the heriot being, as in former times, the best beast, or failing that the best chattel. Quit and free rents of the Manor amounted to £18 per annum, and the market house rent was £3 9s with tolls of £1 per annum. The lord also had the right of nomination of the five almshouses of the Beresford endowment, which paid no rent, but had an obligation to spend £5 per annum for their upkeep (which was half the cost required), and also had to maintain at his own expense the upkeep of the Market House and the maintenance of Batchworth Bridge. Nevertheless, it was clearly of considerable value, for one of the few remaining court rolls shows that in 1764, a large portion was in the lease of Thomas Weedon, and a plan belonging to Thomas Brown Weedon shows that, when he had it, it contained Catlets, Clements, Dungeons (probably down Johns), Long Hale, Kiln, and Kings Farm, while on the other side of the Common, the Chorleywood estate, and the land of William Belch Esq were also held in copyhold. The latter property consisted of Brumhalls, together with several closes, or pitles of land, containing nearly 30 acres, and a parcel on the north side of the turnpike, concomitant with Childs Farm. Three tenements, 10 acres of Bevers Bush, formerly in the tenancy of Mary Belch, claypits, yards, gardens, barns, the blacksmith's shop in Solesbridge Lane, and one little tenement adjoining it were bought by Joseph White in 1793. William inherited the estate in 1768, shortly before his father John died in 1771.

Of particular interest is the note in the deeds of the Chorleywood estate, which show the manner of conveyance which took place at a manorial court. In this case, the outgoing owner was, of course, only exercising his right of passage to his son so no money exchanged hands on that account, but as in all cases of copyhold, the lord also had an interest. Thus when the court assembled, a twig representing the property was handed to the steward, as a token of its return to the Lord, the property was then proclaimed three times, and on the third call, William came forward to take the title, and pay the requisite fine. Should no-one have come forward, then the property would have reverted to the lord who would then have been free to sell it again.

The plans of the property make clear that Belch's holding consisted of essentially two parts, one to the west of the common land adjoining Station Road, which was made at a relatively recent date, and another to the north of the turnpike and including a part of Solesbridge Lane behind the

Quaker burial ground. The exact details were covered by plans shown at the time of auction when Howard Gilliat owned part. Lot 4, describing the latter portion as consisting of Bevers Bush, a home with pleasure grounds, yards, and out buildings, in all comprising two acres was then tenanted by Seabrook. After the sale it came into to possession of Mr McNamara, FRCS, who kept it until the First World War, when he sold it to the Boultons who, in 1946, sold it to the Baking Research Station.

The copyholds applied, of course, to a great deal of land in both Chorleywood and Rickmansworth, the other two main holdings in Chorleywood being the Cedars estate and the land belonging to the Thelluson trust.

By 1825, when the younger Robert Williams entered Parliament, much had been done to add to the lustre of the Manor of the More (Moor), but the cost became too much. He, therefore, sold it with the Manorial rights of Rickmansworth separately, the latter passing fairly quickly through the hands of first John Alliston, then William Windale, William Dimes, and his son William Piercy, and then to John Saunders Gilliat, who held them for a considerable period before leaving them to his son, Col Babington Gilliat. Then in 1913 the Cedars estate and the Manor were bought by the Darvell family, and part was sold off to the Metropolitan Railway.

The Darvells had thoughts of developing the land, particularly along the Drive, and had invested a great deal of money in their purchase. Unfortunately, war broke out, and apart from the cutting of some firs for the construction of pit props, they were unable to realise any income. Following the war, Henly Batty bought off them the mansion of the Cedars, with adjoining grounds, (which he gave to the National Institute to the Blind), conditionally with the manorial rights, and the Council bought much of the land in the Highfield Way for resale, with covenants to control their development. The sale of the Cedars was completed in 1917. At that time, the Battys lived at the home farmhouse of the meeting place, opposite the Church, now known as the Manor House.

The Chorleywood House estate has already been mentioned in connection with Belch's holdings and the Common, and is now owned by the Council, but its separate history dates back to about 1704, when it consisted of two farms, both held by a yeoman of Watford, one Samuel Ewer, who had mortgaged them for £411 to James Cutler. These were Home Farm, and the Meeting-House Farm, the latter having been used by the Quakers, who disapproved of headstones, and buried their dead quietly in consecrated ground at the back of what is now the Manor House. Then, in the tenth year of Queen Anne, or 1724, depending on whether one takes the written or subscribed date to the deed, a decree of foreclosure was made by the High Court of Chancery, whereby all rights of redemption affecting the said premises became barred.

The property was then bought by John Hobart and Peter Campbell of London, gentlemen related by marriage, who left the combined property to Edward Hobart. Edward's son appears to have been a bit of a lad, for his father cut him off with the traditional one shilling, leaving the whole estate to Anne, who carried it in marriage to Ralph Wilson. He sold off Meeting House Farm to his brother-in-law, John Winfield, sharing the use of the barns and farm machinery. In 1756, the estate was once again re-united, when it was jointly left to George Winfield Wilson, a Captain of the East India Co, who left it to his wife Harriet who died in 1789, and then to his daughter Jane. Jane died in 1811, leaving £40,000, some of which went to a number of beneficiaries, and the land and buildings to her nephew George Thompson and his wife Letitia, who lived with her. They promptly sold it to William Dawes, who left it to his son John, who in turn sold it to John Barnes in 1822.

John Barnes was a wealthy stockbroker, who at one time lived at Sunshine House (later the first Sunshine House for Blind Babies, which was burnt down and then rebuilt by the Rymans), and is thought to have moved to Two Gables, before buying the Chorleywood estate. After the sale, he renewed the covenant regarding the small piece of commonland between it and the estate, which had been allowed to lapse, and then built the large Mansion, which stood there when Lady Ela bought the property. John left it to his two sons, Henry and Charles who, after running into financial problems, let it the banking firm of Cazenove, and then sold it to Howard Gilliat, a cousin of John Saunders, who also owned land at Ripton Hall, Huntingdon where, after three years, he returned, leasing it to George Robinson.

The sale plan at that time described it as consisting of a mansion called Chorleywood House, buildings, coach-houses, stables, cottages, and gardens, pleasure-grounds, parkland, and land covered with water, in all 250 acres 1 rood and 22 perches, or thereabouts. On 29 May it changed hands again, when it was resold to Major Fontanblanque Cox, (a biographer, and great rider to hounds), who lived there till 1892, when he sold it to Lady Ela Russell for £30,000. Lady Ela sold a part un-named, to Arthur Herbrand Russell for £4,000, and bought a number of tenements in Solesbridge Lane, and then, dissatisfied with the Mansion, pulled it down, leaving two charming oils of the original house painted by her and marked with the date of their destruction as 1898. Lady Ela was a sister of the Duchess of Bedford, and a generous benefactor to the district, though she preferred to worship at Chenies, and her name recurs repeatedly in the twentieth century in connection with various works, though in private life she was of a retiring disposition, a prim little figure, well endowed with those natural gifts which the family have so often displayed.

When she died, she left it to her sister, Lady Romola Russell, who decided to reside there for six months before deciding between Chorleywood and Ampthill, after which she returned to her original home and sold the estate to the Darvells, excluding the Manor House, which she sold to Mr Batty. Then at the outset of the second World War, they sold it to the Council for the generous figure of £5,000, excluding the parkland, which was bought by means of grants, for £16,000 — grants given respectively by Hertfordshire and London. Architecturally, the later Mansion is not a patch on the original, but the internal layout, with its spacious and comfortable parqueted floors, and the magnificent wood carvings which surmount the panelled hall, are a credit to the Darvells who completed its construction.

A sale plan in Cussans shows the Cedars extending south of the turnpike, from Bury Park to Dog Kennel Lane (so-called because the Arklow hounds were originally kept there, near the corner of the pike). 252 acres, 3 roods, and 22 poles in all, it consisted of a mansion, two lodges, a bailiff's house, outbuildings, a yard, pleasure-grounds, kitchen gardens, plantations, paddock, a home meadow, 11 cottages, a grove, Greenhills Wood, Ashpits Wood, and numerous other copses and fields. It also extended to the south of the pike at Appletree Farm and, to the north, to include Wyatts Farm with two fields adjoining.

The earliest record occurs in 1692, when it was shown in the possession of Thomas Marriott. The Marriotts still had it in 1738, and probably till 1747, when it was bought by the Rt Hon William Finch, who permitted the corner of Constables Cottage to be turned into an ale bar, when it was renamed the Finch's Arms. Finch died in 1774 leaving the property to Lady Charlotte Finch, and in 1775 to Lord Winchelsea, a scion of Sir Moyle Finch, who was created a baronet in 1611, and married Elizabeth Heenage, who was made Viscountess Maidstone and Winchelsea in 1623, whereupon the Finch's Arms was renamed the Winchelsea Arms in her honour.

The Cedar estate was then sold in lots, Appletree and Wyatts Farms being bought by William Morris, who left it to his son Edmund, who then sold it to John Saunders Gilliat who had bought the remainder, and added the Manor, acquired from Robt Williams Junior.

Gilliat was 31 when he made his first purchase in 1860, the grandson of a merchant concerned in the tobacco trade of Kentucky, and it is claimed that his purchase of the estate followed only one transaction of his extensive business. John managed the London office, and his brother Thomas the American side, buying, selling and shipping the product back home. Things had certainly changed since James I, who detested smoking, and ordered that any caught taking snuff should have their noses cut off. John Gilliatt was, to quote George Bastin, well versed in the three R's essential for progress in the City, being rich, respectable, and religious. John was born and brought up in Clapham, which he represented in the House, and schooled at Harrow, with which school he kept a close connection. He also belonged to the so-called Clapham Sect, which included the Babingtons and the Wilberforces, people of a Liberal outlook, and he married a Babington, a relative of Lord Macaulay.

John Saunders left the whole of his estate to his son, Col Babington Gilliat, who then sold it as described. But the family association continued, for Rev H. G. Gilliat had the living at Christchurch till recent memory. Like other men of the period, John Saunders was a great doer, and his name also recurs repeatedly in his work for the community and, like others, he pulled down the original Mansion and rebuilt the present house, which forms part of the School for unsighted and partially sighted girls. Inside, the rooms bear the same stamp of comfort and spaciousness which we associate with Chorleywood House but, like other Victorian buildings, its lines and hideous yellow brick, while serviceable, detract from the natural spleandour of its Cedars of Lebanon, which are truly magnificent. To those of us who have the gift of sight they are perfectly splendid, and one wonders how much the wonderful girls who are educated there can appreciate them.

Apart from the grand estates of Chorleywood, the Cedars, and Loudwater, there were several other large holdings in the Chorleywood section of the Manor of Rickmansworth. Thomas Weedon held, for example, the farms of Catlets, Clements, Hole Farm, Kiln Farm, Kings Farm, and Hall Farm. There was the Berkhamsted poor estate, and the Thelluson trust.

Peter Thelluson was the son of the Ambassador to the Court of Louis XV from Geneva, who settled in London in the middle of the eighteenth century and amassed a great fortune. In 1761, he married Anne Woodford, who bore him three sons, Peter Isaac, his heir, and George and Charles. To each he left large sums, and a residue of £4,500 and properties of £600,000 to be invested in the lives of his sons for their heirs. The will was contested in the House of Lords, and was confirmed, but led to an Exclusion Act whereby such future accummulations were forbidden. In 1806, Peter Isaac was created a Baron and in due course, his son was made Viscount Rendlesham.

Apart from his other holdings, Rendlesham owned in Chorleywood, Bullsland Farm, let to Mr Taylor in 1806, Hill Farm, which was let to John Sedgwick, and Montfichets, let to William Swain.

Almost the only land in Chorleywood, other than Blacketts Farm, now left unaccounted for is what later became the Station estate, a largish parcel of land, including Old Farm (which stood in recent years where the Churleswood Garage is now), covering the whole of Lower Road, with the railway to the north, Hole Farm to the west, and Quickley Lane to the east, to the south of Blacketts. Blacketts was the oldest known holding in the area, dating to 1239, when it was known as Blackethide, situated where Dove Park is today, and in its time probably 120 acres in extent.

It was bought by Elizabeth Craddock to provide an income for the poor of Berkhamsted, probably in the early eighteenth century, and originally included the Hop garden, the Hubbards, the Collyers, and Crab Tree Close; thus it ran along the Bottoms, the lowest part of the Chiltern foothills, and included Currants Bottom, the crossroad at the bottom of Shire Lane where it meets with Lower Road and runs along Mainway, now known as Whiteland Avenue, through Lower Road to Chorleywood Bottom.

In 1894 it was bought by James Beckley, a Baptist, the money then being invested for poor relief. Beckley sold it in small portions, covenanting that none but Baptist churches be built thereon. He laid out the land with the aid of a common labourer, dividing it along Station Road, later renamed Berkshire Hill, and South Road.

His parsimony in this respect left him with a parcel of backland at the Ferry which he was unable to develop. The Ferry received it name because it was at the low point of Lower Road, and invariably flooded after rain, which caused a local wit to chalk the Ferry on its gate. However, in the sixties, this proved an unexpected boon for, by that time, the congestion in Lower Road was a cause for major concern and in discussion with the County and the Police, the Council found it impossible to act unless they could provide alternative parking facilities. It is difficult to think of a more improbable site for a car park than that, but there was no alternative site to use, the building yard near Walkers store being too small to be effective. Consequently, the Ferry was bought and pulled down to provide access to the Old Orchard and, despite contrary public opinion, was turned into a car park.

In defence of the Council's decision it must be borne in mind that a considerable traffic hazard existed. One small boy had been badly hurt while peering out between parked vehicles, when trying to cross the road. The problem was exacerbated by the large vans which were used to supply Walkers, and even more by the builders' merchants, which then opened into Lower Road, and has only recently been vacated. To make matters worse, there were of course vehicles owned by shopkeepers, and commuters who parked there for long periods, seriously restricting room for shoppers. Once the car park was opened, it was possible to restrict waiting periods, which obviated one nuisance, and close off other dangerous areas, so that the end result, while not ideal, is at least tolerable, and crossing is not quite the problem it was.

Beckley's lack of investment in expert advice therefore, had a beneficial result, and his generosity to the Church is notable, for not only did he provide ground in Hillside Road for one, but he also gave a substantial gift towards its construction costs.

As might be expected, the persistence of the names of older places is not always easy to ascertain, particularly in somewhere like Chorleywood, where there has been so much development, but some can be easily identified. Blackethide is still remembered at Blacketts in Dove Park, Clements Farm, Chorleywood Bottom, Hill Farm, Catletts, Colliers (Colleyland), Currants Bottom, Kings End Farm, Hall, Bullsland, and Appletree Farms are all well known and can be easily placed from the map of 1805. Similarly, Loudwater is obviously derived from Lowdewater; the Cedars retains its name, as does Chorleywood House and, though Two Gables is no more, two houses now replacing the one former holding, it can be found, for one of them still bears the name. Why Younger's Farm became the Retreat is not known, and the land (an original tithe), has now given way to a council development, but the house remains as a protected building and the full extent of the original tithe or tenth of a hide holding near the footpath from the Bottom to Clements Road is well known.

The 1735 survey reflects the various sub-tenants' names in both Chenies and Chorleywood, such as Gearies, Cooks, Wyburns, Chilterns, Blacketts, Carpenters, and Collyers.

In Chenies there is Holloway Lane, once Holywell Lane, and at various periods there are other references to the well, such as Holywell fields, St Mary Crofts and its spring called 'Maydenwell', but the site is unknown. Close to the lane leading to Mountwood Farm are Lamb Croft and Loves Croft, the former being called Lamp Croft in the thirteenth century, because its tenant was responsible for lighting the altar of St Mary within the church in time for Mass, and the former starting as Loaves Croft, its tenant having the duty to supply bread for the Lammas day celebration of the harvest.

The farms at Green Street were known after their holders too, Little Green Street Farm being called Tylers in the 14th century, and Great Green Street Farm, Graces. The farmhouse site next to the cricket pitch was known as Wyburns, while the cricket pitch was once Brickells, close to Claypits, from which the raw material for construction was probably taken, roughly near the present Garden Centre.

The oldest known road was, of course, the St Albans-Silchester road, which roughly followed North Hill and passed between the villas, across the head of Whitelands Avenue and continued towards Roughwood Park, touching Phillipshill Farm. By Saxon times the main track between

Rickmeresworth and Agmondesham must also have been constructed, together with Shire Lane, and Quickley Lane, but to call them roads is a misnomer, for they were little more than small Saxon tracks. In fact, in later centuries, the state of the main road between Hatfield and Reading was so bad that it could not take a coach. Accordingly, a petition was made to the House of Lords for the widening and making up of the road on 16 January 1768. Some 400 trustees undertook its maintenance, among them Ambrose Austin of Solesbridge, John Body of Chenies, the Drakes of Shardeloes, and others well-known hereabouts, such as Thomas Dell, J. Dodd, Charles Lowndes, the Shrimptons, and Josiah Simpson.

Agreement for the making up of the Turnpike was finally reached when the Act of 17 March 1768 received Royal assent. The road eventually became known as the Gout Track, as it was habitually used by the Marquess of Salisbury, to travel between Hatfield and Cheltenham or Bath, for relief in the waters. From a relatively early time, there was another road linking the Manor of Chenies to the turnpike, and continuing to the farms of Green Street. This road doubtless continued to Chorleywood, certainly after the arrival of the Metropolitan line, though probably earlier.

ABOVE: Catletts Farm, now Catlipps, and BELOW: Youngers Farm, later
the Retreat, home of Robt Turney.

ABOVE: The Old Shepherd, next to Shepherd Cottage; CENTRE: the Forge Cottage, site of the Smithy, and BELOW: Bullsland Farm.

ABOVE: Hall Farm, which still retains its Tudor oak beams in the bedrooms; BELOW: Boultons, now the Flour Milling and Baking Research Station.

ABOVE: Front view of Old Chorleywood House, pulled down 1882, and
BELOW: Chorleywood House as built for Lady Monica Ela Russell in 1885.

ABOVE LEFT: Park view of Chorleywood House; RIGHT: the carved staircase; BELOW LEFT: the Rockery, with the Drill Hall behind, and RIGHT: Robt Stacey with the greenhouse staff.

LEFT: The Hardens at the Fishery bridge; CENTRE: the Fisheries, rebuilt to its original design after the fire; BELOW: the sluice beneath the pump house of Chorleywood House grounds, (EVP) and RIGHT: the engine of the pump house. (EVP)

LEFT: Chorleywood House Lodge; BELOW: the Cedars, now the Blind School for unsighted and partially sighted girls, given to the RNIB by Henly Batty; ABOVE RIGHT: Constables Cottage, once the Finch's and then the Winchelsea Arms, and CENTRE: the Reading Room, Cedars Estate.

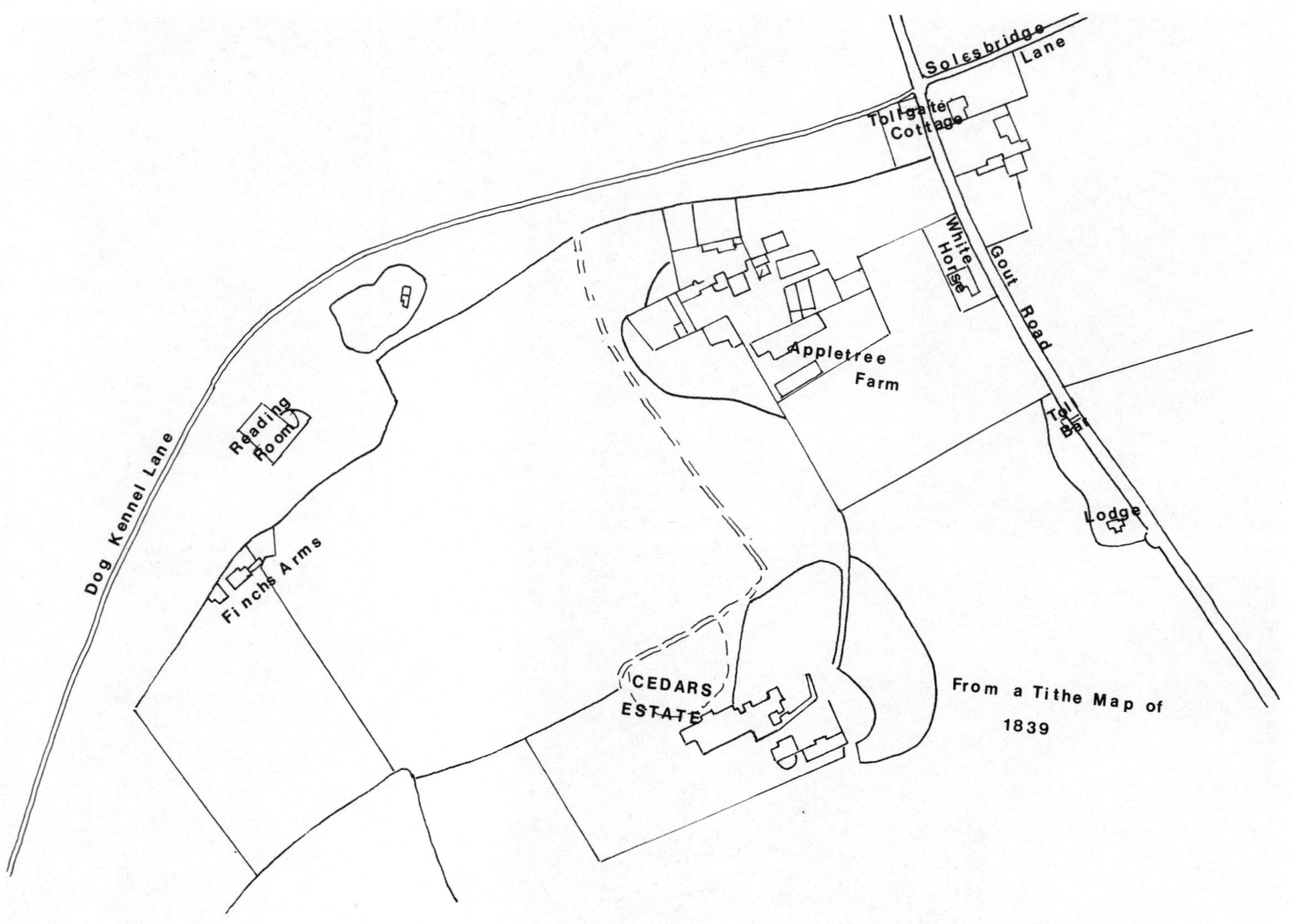

The Tithe Map of part of the Cedars Estate, showing the site of the Toll Bar.

LEFT: Appletree Farm, home of Sir Henry Wood; RIGHT: South Road
before making up, CENTRE: The Cedars Almshouses; and BELOW: early
20th century wedding under the incumbency of Rev Gilliat.

ABOVE: Station Road, now Berks Hill, named after the Berkhamsted Poor Estate; INSET: the Chorleywood Hotel, 1900, when the Berkeley Arms moved there from the Hammer, Station approach: meeting place of the Masonic Lodge and the Round Table; BELOW: Station Approach.

ABOVE: The shops, Station Approach; BELOW: the Rose and Crown,
named after Rose's Tea Rooms.

ABOVE: Old Farm, and Currants Bottom; LEFT: Shire Lane from the bridge, c1914; CENTRE: Station Road, Darvells Corner; BELOW: Chorleywood West; OPPOSITE ABOVE: Colleyland, originally Collier's field, part of the Berkhamsted Poor Estate; and BELOW: deed showing grant of lands to Thomas Weedon.

The Manor of Rickmersworth in the County of Hertford, to wit } The View of Frankpledge with the Court Baron of Henry Fotherley Whitfield Esquire Lord of the said Manor holden in and for the said Manor on Wednesday the Twenty second and Thursday the Twenty third day of April in the Year of our Lord one thousand seven hundred and Sixty seven Before Thomas Groome Gentleman Steward there Amongst other things It is thus Enrolled,

At this Court the Lord of this Manor upon the humble Petition of Thomas Weedon of Wilkind within this Manor one of the Customary Tenants of the said Manor out of his Special Favour Granted his Licence to the said Thomas Weedon to Demise and Let All That Messuage or Tenement with the Barns Stables Outhouses Yards Gardens and Orchards thereunto belonging called Clements And all those Closes of Land called Nodes fields divided into two Fields or Closes And Containing together by Estimation Ten acres more or less One other Field called Homefield Containing by Estimation seven acres and an half more or less One other Field called Doll Field also divided into two Fields or Closes And Containing together by Estimation ten Acres, more or less And all that Spring of Wood Containing two acres and an half more or less And a rightle adjoining thereto And also the two Orchards thereunto adjoining Containing by Estimation two acres and an half To all which premisses the said Thomas Weedon was Admitted at a Court Baron held the seventeenth day of April one thousand seven hundred and forty five on the Surrender of Isaac Junge and his Wife Theretofore made To the Use of Solomon Weedon since deceased late Father of the said Thomas Weedon for his Life With Remainder To the said Thomas Weedon and his Heirs All Which Clifs Lands and premisses are situate lying and being in Charley Wood Hamblett in the parish of Rickmersworth and holden of this Manor and now are in the occupation of Daniel Swain or his Undertenants Or any part or parcel thereof to any person or persons from the Feast day of Saint Michael the Archangel now last past for any Term or number of Years not exceeding Twenty one Years thence next ensuing Reserving nevertheless to the Lord of this Manor All Heriotts Fines Rents Services and Customs heretofore due and of Right Accustomed And so that the Houses Outhouses Hedges Ditches Fences and other the premisses with the appurtenances from time to time well and sufficiently repaired and amended And the Heriotts Fines Rents Charges Suits Customs and Services thereupon due to the Lord and of Right accustomed be well and sufficiently made tendred and paid Otherwise this Licence to be Void. Examined by me

Thos. Groome Steward

LEFT: St Michael's Chenies; RIGHT: rear view of St Michael's and graveyard; CENTRE: the Vicarage, Chenies; BELOW: the original Christchurch.

The Church Manifold

The parish of Chenies derived from the manor, and the Church of St Michael is thought to have been built originally by Alexander de Isenhampstead. The Manor House itself has been well preserved, but contains little of the original material, remaining with the Bedford family who, through marriage, held it of the Cheyne family until well into the 20th century, when it was sold to Alistair Macleod Matthews. The village still retains much of its former layout, as can be seen in a survey map of 1735.

Of the original glass in the church, only a portion remains, bearing the arms of the Russell family, most of the early stained glass having been removed to Woburn. The Church itself consists of a chancel, organ chamber, nave, north aisle, south porch, and west tower, built of flint with stone dressings, roofed with tiles. The present Church dates to about the 15th century, when it was rebuilt on the site of a 12th century edifice, the only remains of which are the font and a capital both in the south aisle. The north, or Bedford Chapel was rebuilt in 1556, and enlarged in 1906, while in 1861, and 1887, the whole building was extensively restored; the organ chamber and porch are modern. The south doorway and the two windows are late 15th century work, much repaired, and the tower consists of two stages with an embattled parapet.

The Bedford chapel is entirely modern, but it has two wooden images of late 16th century work and, in the west, some carved angels of the 17th century, holding shields with the Russell arms, and there are four funeral helms. On the west, corresponding to the south arcade, is a brass with the figure in Mass vestments of Richard Newland, the rector, (who died in 1494), carrying an inverted inscription, and to this have been added many other sculptures, brasses, and details, which portray the rich lustre of the family history, from Agnes and John Cheyne on to this century, and over which ring out the six bells designed by Mears of London, set up in 1826.

The ancient parish of Rickmansworth consists of mixed land, moorland, park and woodland, several manors, many farms, and the small market town of Rickmansworth, in which many acres of commuter land have been developed, bringing the present population to about 16,000. It was not rated as a distinctive parish until after the Dissolution, as it was then held of the Liberty, but for purposes of tithe, it was established in 1219, when Pope Honorius III confirmed its gift to the sacrist of St Albans at the time of Abbot Geoffrey. The original church no longer exists, having been replaced by the Church of Our Lady, of which the oldest part is the tower built in 1630. It has eight bells made by Lester and Pack of London, which were hung in 1765, and were said to have been recast from five heavier bells which hung in the church in 1552.

In all, the ancient parish consisted of 9,449 acres, of which the Manor of the Moor seems from an early period to have had an individuality of its own. It extended from Northwood to Chenies in one direction, and from Watford to Denham and the Chalfonts in the other. In practice, this vast parish could only be manageable while the population remained small, and even then many remained without its ministry for the simple reason of distance. Distances from small villages, such as the Swillett, and Chorleywood Bottom, were too far for the old, the sick, and the very young to walk, and though a ten mile walk was not thought out of the way for the young and fit, it was obviously a limiting factor.

Nevertheless, Rickmansworth's very proximity to the capital, and to St Albans, attracted many from London, especially during the Bubonic Plague. Apart from these times of crisis Rickmansworth was near the court which often met at the Moor, Kings Langley, and St Albans. After the Civil War, its never-failing charm again attracted men of means, made wealthy as the result of the exploitation of the Indies and the American colonies, a feature reinforced at the end of the nineteenth century as the railway was extended.

The latter development, added to the rectitude prevalent during Victoria's reign, caused three men of Chorleywood to build a new Church for people living in Chorleywood. They were James Hayward, John Barnes, and William Prowting Roberts. Roberts was a Radical who lived at Heringsgate House, near the farm of Herringers, who strongly advocated trade unionism. Accordingly, these three petitioned the Lord Bishop of London, appropriator of the great tithes of Rickmansworth, and the patron of the vicarage, James Weld the Bishop's lessee, and Rev Edward Hodgson, Vicar of Rickmansworth, to build and endow a church on the Common, known as Chorleywood Common, by a letter submitted on 15 August 1840. The application was made on behalf of themselves as subscribers, who were prepared to build and endow the new church, because 300 persons in this area resided upwards of two miles from any existing church, and within one mile of the proposed site. It was agreed that they would lay out £1,050 for the building of the church, and a further £1,000 as an endowment. Further, they requested that the advowson be given to James Hayward. Their request was granted, and the new church was consecrated on 13 November 1845. The new parish was created on 3 December of the same year by Order in Council, which ceded the new parish of Loudwater, the Cedars and so on, from the original parish of Rickmansworth.

Other parishes soon followed:— West Hyde in 1846, Northwood in 1854, Croxley in 1872, and Mill End in 1875.

The original church was designed in the English style by B. Ferry FSA, and consisted of a nave, chancel, vestry, and tower (which still remains) capped with a small pointed roof. It was rebuilt in 1870, and completed in 1871, the small capped roof being later changed to a spire. Services were conducted in the adjoining small church school during the rebuilding.

In the interim the Chartists had bought the farm of Herringers, and Prowting Roberts enlisted the aid of John Saunders Gilliat and Rev Arthur Scrivenor to build a small daughter chapel there, to which end they subscribed £252 3s 0d, after which, with one exception, it became self supporting, but was lost to Chorleywood when the new Parish of Chalfont St Peter, Mill End, was created in 1865.

There were, of course, other changes: the parishes of Rickmansworth, Chorleywood, etc, were conveyed in 1852 from the See of London to the See of Rochester, and later, when the new See of St Albans was constituted, they were conveyed once more back to St Albans. In 1853 the small church school was added and a vicarage, c1869-1870, at the expense of John Saunders Gilliat. Further, when James Hayward left the district, the advowson was given to Gilliat and then transferred to the Church Pastoral Aid Society Board of Patronage.

The new Church was designed by Mr Street ARA who added buttresses to the tower and rebuilt the remainder; it was re-consecrated in 1870 by the Bishop of Rochester. It received 48 offertories, among them a beautiful brass lectern designed by Mr Street, and given by Mrs Fitzgerald, a Bible in two volumes subscribed by the poor of the parish, a pair of brass candlesticks given by Rev Aitken and his wife, a stone altar piece given by Rev J. Barnes in memory of his mother, and stained glass windows by the Barnes family. The painted and illuminated chancel roof was gifted by George Robinson, and the silver gilt altar by John Gilliat.

To begin with, the music for services was supplied by an harmonium, but about 1881, when the spire was added, and the clock in 1882, an organ was subscribed and purchased.

By this time population growth as a result of the railway extension had increased congregations, and the provision of a further church became essential. Beckley's covenant made the Station Estate inaccessible, but Gilliat, not to be denied, bought a plot on the other side of Quickley Lane. Then, with money donated by Lady Ela Russell and John Gilliat, the services of Eustace Frere ARIBA were engaged to build an iron frame church there as a daughter church in 1909. By 1920, the population had grown further and the graveyard of the original church had to be extended. Thus in 1921, new land was added and walled off to prevent grazing among the headstones. Access was provided to the yard through a splendid lych gate given by Mrs S. G. Barnes in memory of her husband. The consecration took place on 29 July 1921, when the service was conducted by Rev Cecil Hodges.

In the early part of the 1950s the then Urban District Council concluded that there was a need for a Lawn Cemetery of Remembrance, a pretty walled garden which stands within the Chorleywood House grounds just to the right as one enters the main park, where people could buy small plots. The Bishop of St Albans agreed to bless it but suggested that a part be reserved for Catholics. The Catholic incumbent of the time, however, took the view that a blessing by an Anglican was of no concern to his flock, and suggested that the Bishop bless the whole, as they would do in turn when the matter arose, and so it worked out.

Christchurch also owns a small plot of ground in Highfield Way which was given them by the Metropolitan Estate, bought from the Cedars, but the new and more important Parish of St Andrews had still to be formed.

It was clear by 1963 that for the new Parish to be built land would have to be added and, by the generous co-operation of the neighbouring parishes, it was: part coming from the See of Oxford within Bucks. In 1965, the Bishop of Bedford laid the foundation stone and in 1966, the new church built by Messrs Gulletts of Chorleywood was consecrated by the Bishop of St Albans. This church was in contrast; built to modern design, rectangular in shape, in redbrick, with a tiled pitched roof, it has one small bell hung over the main entrance to the west. The arrangement of the altar along the length of the Church gives a greater feeling of participation. Its first incumbent was Rev John Perry, and is now the Right Rev Bishop Pytches.

Christchurch and School with Lych Gate.

ABOVE: The Church of Our Lady, St Mary of the Island, vandalised during the time of Wolsley — the original Parish Church of Rickmansworth and Chorleywood; LEFT: the Old Vicarage, Christchurch, and RIGHT: the new one. OPPOSITE ABOVE: The daughter Church at Heronsgate, subscribed by patrons of Christchurch; CENTRE LEFT: the Iron Frame Church of St Andrews, now the Church Hall; RIGHT: St Andrews today; BELOW LEFT: the Vicarage, St Andrews, and RIGHT: St John Fisher, Shire Lane.

LEFT: The Baptist Chapel, Chenies; RIGHT: the Baptist Chapel, Chorleywood; BELOW: the Manse, Chenies.

Different Causes

Locally, the first note of the revitalised Puritan movement which follows Lollardy, was struck when John Knox paid a visit to Amersham, in 1553, to preach a most outspoken sermon on the accession of Mary.

In Chenies it was the Baptists who led the way, the Presbyterian rector of St Michael, Benjamin Agas, being ejected in 1662. However, by 1705, two cottages outside the Bedford holding in Chenies were licensed as meeting-houses, and there is a record in one, which shows the affinity of Presbyterians, Independents, and Baptists. It reads, 'upon an impartial confession that they are not ignorant for want of searching, of Believers in Baptism', ie total immersion, they should be admitted to service.

The Russell family provided many of the church's incumbents, some of radical tendencies. Master Allibond got into trouble for refusing to wear a surplice. Wriothesley Russell reported in 1669 that there were no known Dissenters in the village, while he was well aware of, and sympathised with its strong Baptist affiliation.

There were the usual entries, particularly in the time of Master Allibond, of dereliction, and non-payment of tithes. Allibond himself was hauled before the Church court for trespass and for keeping five unringed pigs. Among his congregation, too, were the odd bad hats, such as Thomas Balson, the tailor's son, who died before he was sentenced, and a certain master Jaye.

The first two dissenting ministers in the two meeting-houses which adjoined the later Chapel were James Newton, 1705, and James Cannon, 1708. In 1757, Mr Bennet, probably encouraged by the Bedford's steward, William Davis, moved from St Albans to Chenies, and in 1760 a church was formed by 23 persons, the first entry in the church book being a carefully written confession of their faith, in 24 articles, the original confession of faith beginning, 'We the People of God, Meeting together at Green Street, Chenies in Bucks'.

Green Street was at that time a small hamlet comprising Great and Little Green Street Farms on the turnpike, and the almshouses built by the Countess of Warwick in 1605, and pulled down circa 1865. On 1 February 1773, a lease was granted for a site for a more permanent building, being part of an orchard then rented by George Cooper. The building started in 1778 and was certified to the Eastern Association of Baptist Churches as open for worship on 8 October of that year. The formal vesting of the property took place the following year, though the adjacent cottage, which was occupied by George Cooper, remained for the time in the property of John Davis, until it was converted into the present Manse. In 1779, the Chapel was enlarged at the front and the galleries added. In 1829, subsidence required the insertion of iron columns, and further renovations were made in 1841-45, and again in 1862. These were supervised by Mr Smith, an architect from London. The expenses were partly paid for by the sale of paintings by Mr Boarder. During the pastorate, a small school was added, which removed to Amersham in 1829, when the incumbency of Lord Wriothesley Russell at St Michael's began.

The isolated character of the district of Chorleywood, with its lonely farmhouses, free from the prying eyes of informers, made it an ideal place in which dissent could flourish. The first mention of it was made in 1670 when Kings End Farm, which was then owned by John Watkins, was used as a meeting-house for Quakers, and it was there that Mistress Butterfield records that William Penn married Gulielma Springett, on 4 February 1672.

Penn was the son of Admiral Penn who had taken Jamaica for England during the time of Cromwell. William was born into the Anglican Royalist tradition, but at Oxford he was influenced by Thomas Loe, and Dr John Owen, an influence which led to his repudiation of Anglicanism and his expulsion.

He was a strong and active personality, and despite his views made many powerful friends, among them the Duke of York, later James II. Exactly why he obtained a grant of land in America at Pennsylvania is not known, but the suggestion is that it was in payment for a loan made by his father to Charles II. At any rate, it enabled him to form a settlement in which his Quaker friends could follow their beliefs without hindrance, though their avowed pacificism and refusal to pay the King's taxes brought him continual trouble. Consequently, he spent his time at home trying to defend the interests of himself and his new settlers.

His name is still hallowed at Chorleywood and Rickmansworth for, after his marriage, he went to live at Basing House, the present Headquarters of the Non-Metropolitan District of Three Rivers, and attended meetings at the Manor House in Chorleywood, which was then a licensed meeting-house for Quakers. The last recorded interment was that of Emmot Skidmore, who died in 1836, and was buried in the burial ground at the rear. This burial ground had lain neglected and forgotten because of the Quaker practice of interment without headstones.

The Quakers originally met at five informal meetings, before establishing themselves as a sect at Jordans, meeting as people who had little more in common than the common fear of God. At first, they were as unruly as other similar sects, and their refusal to pay taxes or defend the King indicates a stubborn robustness of spirit. Locally their name is forever connected with Penn, William Penn School having been named after him. It was at the Mayflower Barn at Jordans, too, that the Blind college first met. Now the Quakers are an abstinent and peaceful sect, more associated with the voyage of the Mayflower, though it is in charitable works such as the Wellcome foundation, that they should perhaps be better remembered.

The next mention of a dissenting meeting-house is that of Blacketts, which was licensed in 1709 for Presbyterians.

From then on it was the Baptists who played the most influential role in the district. In 1794 Blacketts was re-registered as a meeting-house for Baptists, and Hole Farm had already been so registered in 1791. But it was not until 12 April, 1905, that the foundation stone of a church was laid in Hillside Road, on land given by James Beckley. Beneath it Mr Felkin placed a bottle containing a shining new penny, and current issues of the *Baptist Times*, and the magazine of the Rickmansworth Baptist Church. Meeting-houses were very much the rule in Chorleywood, thus the Catholic Church, when it ventured back into the district, met at Rosebank, and then settled at St John Fisher, a little further up Shire Lane, where the Council closed its eyes to the placement of a small garage in front of the building line. This is still a meeting-house, for it is the home of the present incumbent; the congregation has so far been unable to secure land on which to build a proper church.

The laying of the Baptist foundation stone was followed by a prayer of dedication given by Rev J. Stuart, hymns were sung, and attendants were told by the presiding cleric, Rev Colin Bryan, that £670 had already been subscribed and promised. When the church opened three years later it was free of debt. The builder was J. A. Bates, and the architect was H. G. Ibberson, FRIBA. Mr Ibberson designed the church with a view to music being provided by an harmonium, and was heard to say that the addition of an organ was distastrous to its aesthetics. The principal donors were James Beckley, Herbert Smith, and Mr Ibberson who gave much of the lead and copper ornamentation.

In 1934, when Rev Dr Charles Brown retired from the ministry at Chorleywood, the church was offered the handsome sum of £3,500 for some devotional work. Mr Ibberson was once more engaged, and on 29 September 1934, a new hall was added, the Florence Brown Hall, named after the wife of the donor. It consisted of an entrance and school hall, a kitchen and the usual offices, and a billiard room.

Probably the last group of Dissenters to reach Chorleywood were the Methodists, disciples of John Wesley. When they arrived is not known, but an old timber Church in Solesbridge Lane was pulled down in 1894, and cannot have been much older than 50 years at the time, which would place its arrival in the first half of the 19th century. In 1893, it was replaced with a new Church in Colleyland, which closed in 1968.

There was some difficulty in disposing of it, partly because the plot was unsuitable for a domestic dwelling, and partly because the Methodists insisted that it should not go to those who might desecrate it with drink. Eventually, after a public meeting, money was subscribed to a Community Arts Centre, and guarantors were forthcoming, but it was not until it had been some time in occupation that the sale was finally completed.

ABOVE LEFT: The Florence Brown Hall; RIGHT: Old Blacketts, the original Presbyterian meeting house, Dove Park; BELOW LEFT: the original Methodist Chapel in Solesbridge lane — the Donkeygate Cathedral, and RIGHT: the later Methodist Chapel, Colleyland.

ABOVE: Kings End Farm, later Kings Farm, and then when owned by the Hon Arthur Capel QC, called King John's Farm; LEFT: King's Farm from the north-west, and RIGHT: the Upper gallery.

ABOVE LEFT: The room where William Penn married Gulielma Springett; RIGHT: the staircase; BELOW LEFT: the formal garden; CENTRE: the living room, and BELOW RIGHT: the front of King's End Farm.

ABOVE: Old cottages Chenies, and BELOW: the view from .the crest of
Chenies gives some idea of the reason behind the choice of the Manor
House site.

Help for the Helpless

The other main role of parishes from the late 15th century was in the provision of local government, particularly care of the needy, and schooling. The latter involved further building work at Christchurch for, when the Church reached its centennial in 1970, the school was bursting at the seams. To remedy this, a portion of the Cedars land was made available, and schoolwork temporarily transferred to the neighbouring house at Parkfield. The school and vicarage were then rebuilt, and reopened in September 1971.

When the Vestry became the main organ of local government, its unique main duties were the maintenance of highways, provision of poor relief, and the keeping of the peace. The first was the responsibility of the surveyor, the second the work of the priest and his deacons, and the third fell to the office of a constable. All the accounting was done by the Church. Such offices were unpopular since they were unpaid. In addition the members of the Parish were expected to turn out six days a year to work on the roads, though this could be compounded by the payment of a fine of a shilling a day.

Up till the Dissolution the work of poor relief had been mainly carried out by monasteries, and by secular lords, whose generosity continued in many cases well into the present time.

In Chenies, for example, the Duchess of Warwick (a Bedford) gave a group of almshouses at the hamlet of Green Street in 1604, which served until the cost of maintenance exceeded their value, and they were pulled down in 1895. In 1835, the then Duke of Bedford gave a group of workhouses at Claypitts, which were mainly used for children, and were adopted by the Amersham Union. But a few years later, this need disappeared, and the workhouses were then bought back by the Duke and converted into five cottages. In Chorleywood, Elizabeth Craddock bought land for the relief of the poor of Berkhamsted, and Gilliat added two pairs of almshouses in 1881, and 1906. These, of course, are only a few of many examples, although not the last.

The Bedford Almshouses stood diagonally facing north-east towards Chilton Woods, then known as the Almshouse Woods.

Surrounding the Manor House to the south was the slaughter yard, next to Calves Platt; further round to the west gardens, and towards the north-west and nearer to the Church were orchards. Common land lay between the footpath to the north of Mountwood Lane and Holloway Lane. To the west of the presnt Manor House are also some remains of the older wing for, in its heyday, the Manor must have been considerably larger, an inventory showing over a 100 rooms, and 74 chimneys, even then small to hold the retinue of a court, despite the sharing of beds. Long after the main family had removed to Woburn, it remained a residence for lesser members of the family, and the almshouses were added in 1604 by the then Countess of Warwick. Only once thereafter was it to regain some of its former glory, when preparations were made to receive back the women and children, when war threatened between James II and William and Mary. The facings were repaired, chimneys swept and the rooms put in order, but it proved a false alarm and no exodus took place. But, as could be expected from a family such as this, they took good care of their people, and the then Duke of Bedford built a workhouse c1700, on the left of the little road leading to Chenies just beyond the Garden Centre, which was taken over by the Amersham Workhouse Trust.

One particular charity of Rickmansworth which concerned Chorleywood was the Beresford Trust. In 1686, John Beresford built and left six almshouses for the poor of Rickmansworth in the High Street. William Ford added another sum of £100 to buy land for the poor of Rickmansworth forever, which was invested in Haschinworth, part of Parrots Farm Croxley, in all 3 acres, 3 roods and 11 perches, which were subsequently sold to Thomas Hoad Woods for £1,400, the money from the sale being invested in Consols. To this Lady Ann Franklin added a charge to the Moor Park estate of £10 per annum, for the benefit of the Almshouses, which were sited where the present Police Station stands, and the disused lock-up was converted into a wash-house for them. Subsequently, they were bought by the Hertfordshire Constabulary for £400 in 1892, and in 1894 the Charity Commissioners amalgamated all these into one, from which they bought four houses in Bury Lane, on land gifted by Lord Ebury. This left a residue of £1,164 16s 6d which was invested in Queensland stock at 3½%, plus the annual charge of £10. From this sum, a yearly income in interest yielded £50 15s 4d, which was dispensed by the Vicar in weekly sums of 3s 9d to each of the four inhabitants, leaving a small residue for their upkeep, and when a relative of the Clerk left a sum of £55 18s 2d, this was also invested in Consols and brought each incumbent a further sum of 6s 11d per week.

The trustees in 1885 were Charles Augustus Barnes of Chorleywood, and John William Birch of Loudwater and, when Rickmansworth was divided, Chorleywood retained an interest in the appointment of one family. The terms of the Trust state that a person guilty of insobriety, insubordination, breach of regulation, or any immoral or unbecoming conduct, or in receipt of poor relief or suffering from mental illness could be removed, and the dwelling re-allotted. No almsperson could sublet, or allow any stranger to occupy any part without permission of the trustees, and they were expected to be persons of good character, able to maintain themselves by their own exertions.

Apart, therefore, from its ecclesiastic activities, the church formed the hub around which local affairs and social activities flourished. Moreover, with the exception of the small Baptist school at Chenies, it was the Church which provided such schooling as was available. Thus in 1853, eight years after the formation of the Chorleywood Parish, a school was added, whose rooms were used both for education and other social activities. In 1868 Miss Wynch was the school mistress, and drew an annual salary of £45 9s 8d but, since she was uncertificated, she was replaced by a Mr and Mrs Henry Roe, who speedily showed their incompetence both at schooling and playing the harmonium, and were replaced by George Hunter, of St John's Training College.

Both the School and the charities were closely associated, there being in all eight charities, a school fund, a school boot and shoe club, an harmonium fund, a harvest festival fund, and the offertories.

The account for 1868, showed a balance brought forward of £2 2s 9d which, when added to the offertories given at Holy Communion of £46 9s 7d, reached a total for the year of £75 9s 8d. This was distributed as follows:

	£	s	d
Given to the aged sick and distressed	25	17	8
Rice, the difference between cost and sale	4	2	3
Blankets to lend in winter	8	10	5
Grant to Library	1	0	0
Society for the propagation of the Bible	4	17	0
The Church missionary society	4	17	0
Additional curates society	4	2	4
Church building society	7	0	5
Hemel Hempstead Infirmary	6	0	7
Balance brought forward	8	8	6

In a letter accompanying the accounts, Rev Clements wrote that the evening school had been well attended, there being 85 scholars, and an average attendance of 49. He added that the clothing and coal clubs had been working satisfactorily, and many a home that Christmas had been made the more cheerful and comfortable by this means. He also appended a note to the effect that there had been 27 christenings that year, 22 deaths, and 7 marriages.

The Poor Law records at Chenies date from 1720 and follow much the same pattern as at Rickmansworth which date from 1702: repairs to the lock-up or cage, and the stocks, another set of which existed near the corner of the Turnpike and Station Road, on the corner of the Common, fines for dereliction, leywrite, and non-payment of tithes, and notes concerning the annual feast on St Stephen's day which lapsed about 1840. In Rickmansworth it was the Michaelmas Fair which was the great occasion, being held between Bury Lane and Church Street. Here were gathered dunnage stalls for sale of second hand clothing. Local labourers would wander around seeking new employment, and advertising their skills by their head gear. A plait signified a thatcher, or a piece of horse hair a carter, etc and when these fairs were discontinued c1880, a Harvest Festival was substituted at Chorleywood.

This took the form of a short service at the church starting at 2.15, followed by a procession, then games or other entertainment on the Common, followed by a meat tea at one of the grounds of either the Cedars or Chorleywood House. Beer was at first provided, but then discontinued, 'owing to difficulty in regulating the supply'. Parishioners over sixteen were charged a shilling a head and all had to supply a cup, saucer, knife, fork, and plate.

Tithe-collection always formed a problem in a non-conformist area, and the matter is well illustrated by the example of John Johnson, who owned the farm at Further Gate (Dell Farm) from 1782 till 1786. The rentable value of his land was reckoned at £5 8s 0d, and on this he owed a tithe of 9d in the pound, ie roughly 4s per annum. John refused to pay, whereupon the Vicar determined to collect the money in kind and appointed Francis Chappell to assess and collect the dues. The apportionment on fruit, kine and milk proved fairly easy, but they fell out on the subject of fleeces, and his son had to resort to an arbiter after his father's death. In his feud with the Vicar, Johnson sold most of his cows and a great many of his sheep, mainly ewes, but the Vicar, making up his accounts at the end of the feud, reckoned he had got the better of the bargain. He lists as having received 170 quarts of milk, 304 eggs, three lambs, two pigs, cherries to the value of 1s and 6d, apples 33s and 6d, pears 6d, a tithe of 15 lambs and pigs 9s, three calf sucklers, one colt, nine fleeces and a half, and an Easter offering of 2d. Allowing for adjustment over barren and unprofitable land of 10s in all, he realised the sum of £7 9s 4d.

In Chorleywood and Chenies, which remained agricultural until the 20th century, the unrest caused by the Industrial Revolution, the migration to the factories and towns, and the subsequent growth of population and squalor caused little concern, except among the mill-workers. Times were hard, but estates were generally well run, and communications were poor. It followed that, though they were by no means ignorant of unrest elsewhere, after a hard day's labour, and then attendance on their own allotments, they had little enough energy or time to enter into affairs not immediately of their own concern. By comparison, it is interesting to note that among the more wealthy residents active support for reform received encouragement. Undoubtedly, the factor which played the most important role was the increase in population. At the turn of the nineteenth century, there were 73 hereditaments in Chorleywood, and a total population of 447, but by 1841, this had increased to 938, and in Chenies had reached an all-time high of 625. Thereafter, the population of Chorleywood continued to increase steadily, but in Chenies it fell, and only after the coming of the railroad, with the overspill of Chorleywood into the bordering Chenies estates, did it begin to rise again.

Undoubtedly, the disparity between the affairs of the poor and those of the gentry played its part in the subsequent turn of affairs, but the representation in Parliament which was largely a matter of patronage, aroused the greater resentment, constituencies could be bought and sold, and not a few represented small patches of ground and not the voice of the electors. People were demanding a right to vote, and the principle of proportional representation was keenly argued. In Rickmansworth, in the late 19th century, a Lodge of the Workers' Union was established, which sent its delegate to the Trades Union Conference which founded the Labour Party.

One of the more militant movements was the Chartists, which had its greatest strength in the north and the midlands where conditions were worst. One of the best Chartists was the mill owner Owen, who by improving the working conditions of his men, and by investing the profits of his company to improve their homes, at the same time encouraging the growth of co-operatives which could buy and sell competitively, set an example which he hoped would be emulated by many. Some believed that they had no hope but in violent action, for example the Luddites who were named after Ned Lud, supposedly the large hammer used to destroy machinery believed to be responsible for taking jobs away from hungry mouths. Another important Chartist was Fergus O'Connor, and his influence was felt in Chorleywood.

Fergus was born in 1796, at Meath in Dungar Castle, and went on to become a barrister at law. He then became an MP for County Cork, and in 1847 sat for Nottingham, by which time he was an acknowledged Chartist leader, whose aims were set out in a charter of rights. On 10 April 1848, he led a large gathering in a march on London but, becoming alarmed at the possibility of violence, persuaded the crowds to disperse and presented the House with a monster petition. He believed that violence would gain them nothing, and the Peterloo massacre and the subsequent harsh sentences at Tolpuddle proved him right. His answer to their problems was to form a society in which shares could be bought for the sum of £2 10s, in increments of 3d, 6d, or a shilling a week. If, he argued, he could raise a sum of £5,000, he believed he could buy land at £8 15s 0d per acre, sufficient to provide a schoolhouse, and house 60 people, leaving a residue sufficient to provide utensils, and machinery to run them, and enough to sustain them until the first harvests were in. In this way, the lucky owners would make themselves eligible for the vote, and with a rent of £5 per annum could build up further funds with which to buy more land, and so on ad infinitum. At first, he thought he would have little chance of success, but a conference was called to discuss the project. Obviously, only a percentage of shareholders would have any chance of gaining emancipation and, to solve this, he proposed that the lots should be made available by a lottery. The scheme was agreed and speakers were sent forth to spread the idea, which was wildly acclaimed.

Money poured in, and a farm at Herringers, owned by the Putnam family from 1700, which became vacant after the last surviving member, Joseph Putnam, died in 1846, was bought in 1847. Work started immediately, the farm buildings were torn down, 19 acres of woodland were grubbed up, and four roadways were built, after the names of the towns from which the chief shareholders came: Halifax, Bradford, Nottingham, and Stockport. A schoolhouse, with two acres of land, was assigned to a Mr Graves, who was to receive payment in money and kind by the parents of children attending the school. O'Connorville (the Land of Peace and Plenty) was opened officially on 17 August 1847. The opening was a scene of wild enthusiasm, and many came from far and near to attend the ceremony, among them Ernest Jones, the poet, who dedicated to them the following poem:

See in here the cottage, labour's own abode,
The pleasant doorway on the cheerful road,
The airy floor, the roof from storms secure,
And dearest charm of all, the grateful soil
That bears its produce from the hands of toil.

When they arrived, they were met by horses and carts garlanded with ribbons, and a brass band struck up *See the conquering hero comes* and, though tired out by a long journey, they only terminated their research 'When sable clouds of night had spread its mantle o'er their small domains'.

The disaster that ensued had nothing to do with local hostility; on the contrary, the Chartists could not have hoped for more encouragement, many labourers after their own long hours spending much time without pay in aiding the establishment of the small colony. Local farmers, moved by their pitiful efforts and anxious to keep the land in good heart, lent them tackle, and advice. A friendly game of cricket was arranged opposite the gate houses, between the newcomers and the villagers, and every welcome that could be given was given. No venture started so auspiciously, yet it failed, for those long accustomed to an industrial economy, and ignorant of farming, whose wives could not bake bread, or use the skills of the dairy, simply could not adjust, and once their subsistence money had gone, had to admit defeat and return home.

On returning home, they had to apply for poor relief, and the local authorities of their home towns applied to Rickmansworth to defray their expenses, on the grounds that they had been domiciled in and paid rates to Rickmansworth. Rickmansworth could not meet these expenses and had to apply to the Government, who set up a Commission to enquire into the matter and into another four similar estates in much the same straits. They found that the charities' rules had been ignored and that the schemes were therefore illegal.

After the failure of his agrarian reform, Fergus went mad, and after a prolonged illness, died and was buried at Kensal Green. At the subsequent trial he was acquitted of knavery, but accused of folly, a Bill was introduced to wind up the scheme, and the land was sold to the landlord of the Swan Inn at Rickmansworth. Not until the passage of the Representation Act of 1918, was the franchise eventually granted, and then not for women, but women might well have been included, had it not been for their own militancy. Their voice had been heard with sympathy until the suffragette movement got into full swing, but then feelings turned against them. Once again it was ill-judged violence which lost the day, actions such as the burning down of the house at Roughwood Lane, and the provocation of Mrs Pankhurst and others aroused intense indignation. Chorleywood was a centre of suffragette activity, ladies from all classes gathering to hear speeches on the Common and local youths used to cycle round them blowing bugles to interrupt their meetings.

One classic story of the time concerned the daughter of Cllr Tofield, who was elected to the Council in 1913. Amy, with the help of a friend, let loose the roller on the Common, so that it rolled down on to Arklow Kennels where the hounds of the hunt were kept. The roller broke open the door and released the hounds all over the Common. It took several days to round them all up, and the Council were asked to intervene. They decided to ask the Constable, whose name at that time happened also to be Constable, to give Amy a good talking to, and he duly arrived to administer the lecture, but Mrs Tofield got in first with a salvo on the dangers to children of leaving a loose roller on the Common. Amy never received the lecture, poor Constable retiring, thinking that in this case discretion was the better part of valour. Whether it was merely a prank, a reaction to blood sport, or a suffragette act is neither here nor there, but it does show that the ladies of the village were a force to be reckoned with.

ABOVE: Cottage on the corner of Latimer Road, Chenies; the original site of the Goat Inn, and BELOW: the Bedford Arms, to which the Goat transferred.

LEFT: Bedford Arms, rebuilt after the fire; RIGHT: the Old Village Shop, now a private house; CENTRE: listed Tudor buildings, Chenies, showing back lane on the right leading to Mountwood Farm, and Holloway (Holywell) Road; BELOW: the Green and Well, Chenies.

LEFT: Little Greenstreet Farm, and RIGHT: its barn: though in Bucks, it is typical of Hertfordshire barns, such as that at Appletree Farm; CENTRE: the Countess of Warwick's Almshouses, the foundations of which lie behind Little Greenstreet Farm; (MM) BELOW: Claypitts Cottages, built originally as a workhouse for children, by the Duke of Bedford.

LEFT: Newhouse Farm; RIGHT: Stag Lane School; and BELOW: the violin class of 1906, Christchurch School.

ABOVE: Stag Lane School extension: LEFT: the Drill Hall in the Compound, Chorleywood House, now an annexe to the Hertfordshire Field Study Centre; RIGHT: the Civil Defence Centre in the Compound, now the Hertfordshire Field Study Centre, and in between the Poplar Youth Club; CENTRE: Arnett Hill School, the drab exterior belying its excellent record, and BELOW: the Russell School.

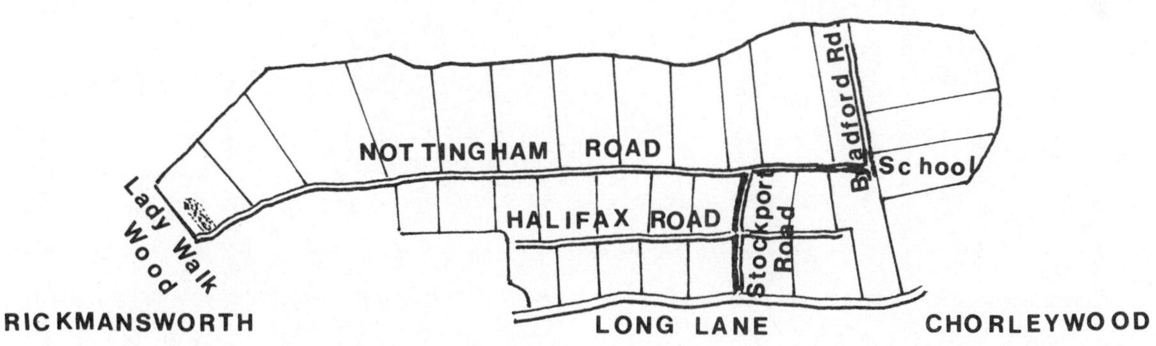

ABOVE: Clement Dane's School; LEFT: Dell Farm, Chorleywood House grounds, once owned by Johnson; RIGHT: the White Horse Inn on the Gout Road; BELOW: The layout of Herringers when it became O'Connorville.

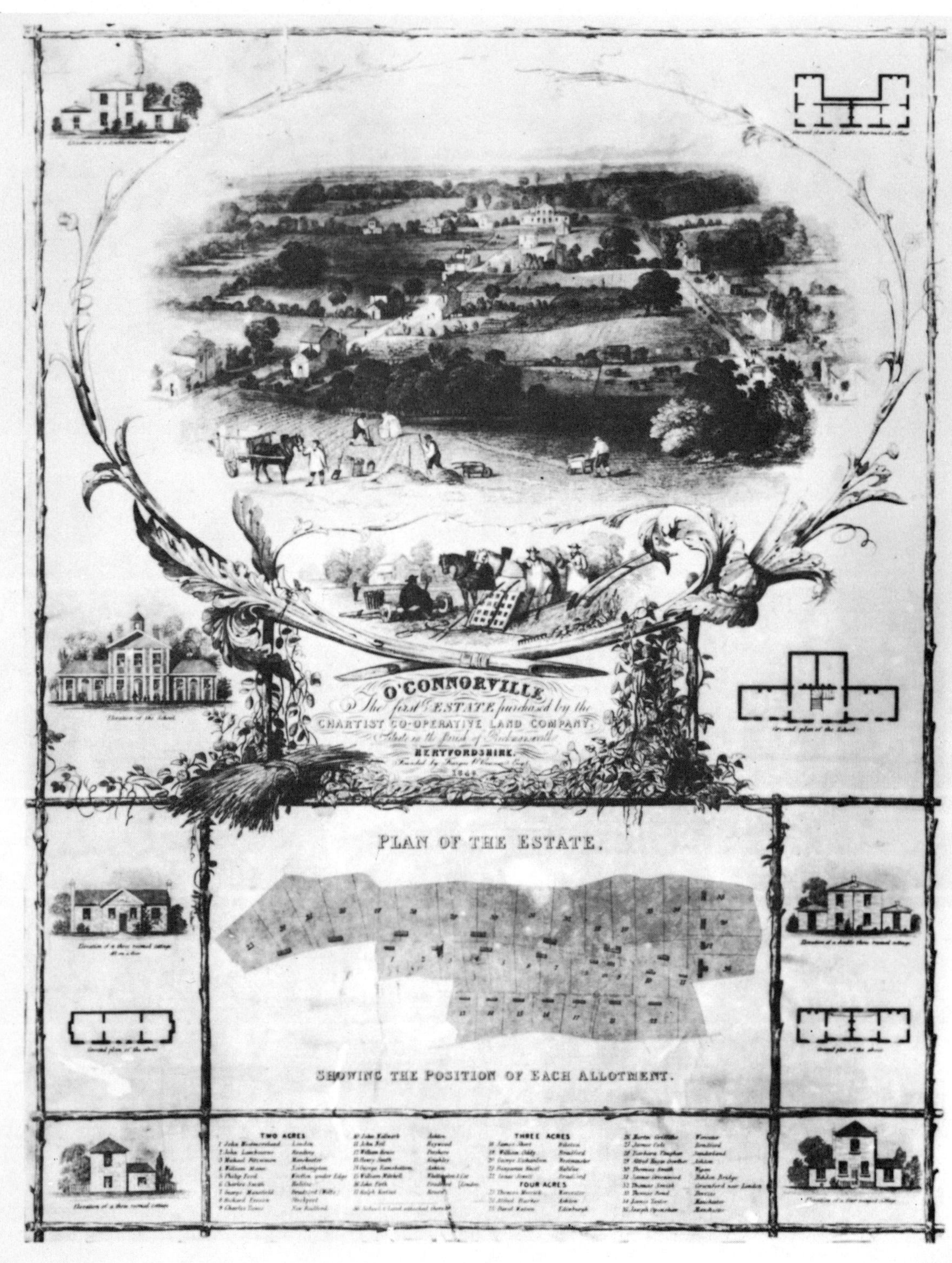

O'Connorville.

LEFT: The advertisement for the sale of O'Connorville at the Swan; ABOVE: the Land of Liberty, Peace and Plenty, set up in defiance of O'Connors' temperance views, and CENTRE: the Stag, opposition in the Swillet; BELOW: Roughwood House, burned by the Suffragettes.

ABOVE: Chenies, looking towards Latimer; BELOW: Chenies, Rickmansworth Road, and the Red Lion.

Wise Counsels

Apart from the old village of Chenies to the north of the A404, Chorleywood, Bucks, and Chorleywood, Herts form in fact one town, but are two communities, separated more by local government and public sentiment than anything else. Moreover, when it comes to matters of use, then even the village cannot be excluded. Thus the residents share the same telephone exchange of Chorleywood, the same water supply, the same sewage system, the same shopping centres, and even belong to common associations. They have a common library, and the one secondary school within the area has its classrooms in Herts and its school grounds and playing fields in Bucks.

However, their areas of local government are quite distinct, though both have their own parish councils, and both belong to non-metropolitan districts: Chenies Parish Council and Chiltern District, and Chorleywood Parish Council and Three Rivers District. The separation is governed by the line of the County boundary, and little else, but both counties jealously guard their own and, when a merger was suggested at the last county boundary revision, the thorny subject was dropped. Of the two authorities, Chorleywood is the largest and has the more complex history.

Following the introduction of the Local Government Act of 1894, a letter was sent to the Hertfordshire County Council couched in the following terms:
'My Lords and Gentlemen,
'In asking the County Council to cause enquiry to be made into the desirability of forming the ecclesiastical Parish of Chorleywood into a separate civil parish, we the undersigned ratepayers of Chorleywood lay the following statements before them for their consideration.
'Before 1845, Chorleywood was without schools or any place of worship. About 1842, steps were taken to raise funds for the building of a church and school. These have been maintained by voluntary subscription ever since. Water has been laid on to almost every house, and the population has grown to 915 (1891 census). A lending library, postal and telegraphic services are available, and local landlords provide allotments (at fair rentals) whenever these are required. Further the Parish lies some 2½ miles distant from Rickmansworth and contributes two-fifths of the rates of Rickmansworth Council, though it is represented by only two members. Improvments are continually being made within Rickmansworth at the Chorleywood ratepayers' expense, without subscribing anything to the well-being of the district.'
A copy of the letter without signature was found in the scrapbook given by Charles Barnes to Harry Ryman. A letter from the County Clerk to the Peace Officer indicated that the petition was successful, suggested that on the first Monday after 10 March 1898, an election be held, and enclosed an electoral register, together with a note that the Parish boundaries could be inspected at the office of H. Morton Turner of Watford, the Clerk for the Guardians of the Poor of Watford Union.

Notice of the election was given out in church in the manner adopted by the Vestry, and 14 nominations were forthcoming. The names were written on a blackboard, and the chairman, Rev

Cecil Hughes asked the electors present whether they wished to ask any questions of the candidates. No questions being forthcoming, the election proceeded by a show of hands, and the following were elected: Charles A. Barnes, 61 votes; Thomas Brown Weedon (junior), 52 votes; John Pullen, 49 votes; Harry Darvell, 46 votes; James Woods, 45 votes; Arthur J. Bates, 43 votes; John Saunders Gilliat, 43 votes, and George Coster, 41 votes.

Thereafter, the Council met at the Schoolhouse until the formation of the Urban District Council in 1913. The first meeting was held on Saturday 16 April at 3 pm. Mr Barnes was elected Chairman, and Arthur Thomas Guy was appointed Clerk (at a salary not exceeding £10 per annum), while Kelham Sharpe was appointed Treasurer with two sureties of £50 each. Three overseers, Arthur Edward Fox, Arthur James Bates, and Thomas Emery were elected, and Mr Barnes and Mr Darvell undertook the work of the surveyors.

The new Clerk was authorised to buy books and stationery, and a strong tin box. The Council agreed to meet on Mondays at 7 pm and that five clear days' notice be given of each meeting. Then at the second meeting the Council adopted its standing general orders.

Typical of the problems which beset the new Council was that of the Gate pond. The pond lay exactly opposite the Gate Inn, and was used by carters hauling goods along the turnpike to London. Starting at either Reading or High Wycombe, they would usually stop to breakfast and water their horses, but the pond lay on the Common, and the water had become stagnant and foul. Mr Gilliat was willing to have it cleaned, but refused to maintain it on the plea that it was primarily used for customers of the Gate, and that its maintenance was therefore the responsibility of the innkeeper. In turn, the innkeeper argued that it was also used by the public and should therefore be maintained by the Council. After some debate the issue was decided, by eliminating it altogether, by filling it with rubble, and putting it back to grass.

Shortly after the Council was formed, Mr Gilliat found the work too onerous, and sought to surrender his seat, which was then offered to Jack Ryman's father, who had been next highest on the list of votes. Thus began a family association with the Council which, except for a brief period, has continued to this day. In their time, both father and son held the posts of Chairman of the Council, and Chairman of Finance and General Purposes and, when Jack finally retired in 1966, after an association of 65 years, he was awarded the MBE and remained an Alderman of the County. Since then his son Desmond has sought election following Local Government reorganisation, and has in his turn served as Chairman of the present Parish Council, thus continuing the long family tradition.

One of the first tasks of the new Council was to regularise the naming of roads and, following a meeting held on 12 September 1898, the following decisions were made and advertised in the *Watford Observer*: 1. From Pullen's post office on the turnpike (the A404) to the railway bridge at Dungeons — Dog Kennel Road; 2. from the railway bridge to the Chorleywood boundary at Berry Lane — New Road; 3. from the Stag to Shire Lane — Bloomfields Road; 4. from Bloomfields Road to the Common — Quickley Road; 5. from Kings Farm to the Parish boundary — Kings Road; 6. from the railway bridge to the Stag — Quakers Road; 7. from Bloomfields Road, to Currants Bottom (ie the cross road at the bottom of Shire Lane where stood Old Farm, and now stands Churleswood service station) — Shires Road; 8. from Rickmansworth (main) Road to Sarratt Mill — Sarratt Road; 9. from Pullen's post office on the turnpike to the junction of Watford Rural — Solesbridge Road.

Since then, there have been many changes; to begin with the roads were left unsurfaced, dusty in summer, and waterlogged in winter. Even the turnpike was left unflagged until 1914, and the remainder were left until the establishment of a proper sewage system. Bloomfields Road is now Heronsgate Road, New Road is Valley Road, Kings Road, Stag Lane, Quakers Lane has disappeared, and Quickley and Shires Roads have become Quickley Lane and Shire Lane.

In 1889, it was proposed to build another road from the turnpike across the Common to Station Road, and Mr Darvell undertook to raise the funds. Lady Ela gave £100, John Gilliat another £100, but the remaining £100 took till 1905 to be subscribed, whereupon Mr Darvell undertook to build the road for that amount.

In 1899 the County approached the Urban District authority for a precept to maintain the County Constabulary, and towards improvements of County roads, and a sum of £30 per annum was agreed, at that time roughly a 1½d rate.

Fortunately, the Boer campaign had little effect on the district, though the return of Captain Babington Gilliat, who had commanded the 42nd squadron of the Hertfordshire Imperial Yeomanry, was marked by general rejoicing. The villagers turned out to greet him at Rickmansworth station and towed him home along the Drive to the Cedars (now The Drive), in a cart bedecked with flowers, where they partook of a celebratory supper given by his father in thanks at his safe return.

The beginning of the 20th century is also marked by the acceptance of a recognition of secular as well as ecclesiastical responsibility for education. Thus, after the passage of the Local Education Act of 1902, the Council was permitted to appoint one member to the School management committee.

At that time, there was only one school in the district, the privately maintained Church School, where the children learned the three R's, and some aspects of horticulture. Under the new Act the Council appointed John Pullen to the School management committee, which was naturally chaired by the Vicar.

In the election of 1904, there was a tie between Mr Loram, and Mr Butterfield. The chairman *pro tem*, the Vicar, Rev Cecil Hughes, cast his vote in favour of Mr Loram, but said that, if within the next ten minutes five electors voted for a ballot, the decision would be so decided. As only three electors were present, Mr Loram was duly elected.

Feelings ran high, electors regarding the absence of notice and paucity of time as unreasonable. No press notice had been given, and the only indication was on a notice board at the Church. A decision was therefore taken to give press notices in future, and to erect Council notice boards in prominent positions. This stilled the voice of complaint, but made little difference to the number of votes recorded. Much the same is true today; thus when there was considerable agitation to make committee meetings open to the public, (around the '70s) at first perhaps as many as 20 souls out of a possible 2,000 attended and this number soon dropped, so that even in the much larger Three Rivers District it is rare, unless a matter of considerable local grievance is being heard, to get much more than five to ten people out of a possible 16,000, at a meeting, and they have to be excluded half the time.

The next issue to engage the attention of the Council was sewage disposal. In a letter written by the then Inspector of Nuisances, Mr J. Robinson, he said that the Gate Cottages had no means of drainage, slop water, excreta, and refuse, all being deposited in the gardens.

The prevailing view was that cess pools were both easy and cheap to clean, and that the cost of a proper sewage system would be prohibitive, and would rob the soil of much needed nutriment. That this was not the view of the Inspector (whose title changed over the years to Public Health Inspector, and then Medical Officer of Health), is not difficult to understand, and the Council, cognisant of the steadily increasing population, and the lack of even surface water drainage, was torn.

The minutes describe the state of affairs in 1910, when they had a suction plant consisting of two vans with hoses, and pumps, the first being bought in 1906 at a cost of £120, and the second in July 1908, for £108.

'Each van is worked by two horses and two men, at a contract price of £1 per day. During 1907,

439 cess pools were emptied, and 1,020 loads removed, each consisting of 466 gallons, or a grand total of 475,320 gallons . . .'

Visits were made to other authorities to compare schemes, but attempts to impose an outside solution were bitterly resisted. The battle over the sewage brought into being the Chorleywood Owners and Occupiers Protection Association, the forerunner of present residents' associations. This was formed in 1908 and, in making representations on behalf of its members, called attention to the 'deplorable state of Shire Lane', the non-clearance of letters, and the hardness of the water supplied by the Uxbridge and Rickmansworth Valley Water Co. In addition, they made application for negotiations to bring electricity into the district, and asked for a road to link the railway with Chorleywood West. It is clear that included among those making these representations were members of the Council itself, and in two aspects they were successful; thus a link passage between the Station and Lower Road was provided, and the County adopted and made up Shire Lane.

These were, of course, not the only matters to concern the Council; both the provision of gas, and the question of fire hazard were municipal problems, but to solve the sewage question they needed a change of status, and the other matters affected public utilities, which managed areas covering more than one authority. The Post for example had been farmed out from a fairly early period and representations had to be made to the Post Master General, which finally succeeded in establishing a telephone exchange and sub-post office at Chorleywood West in 1905 and 1900 respectively and much later, another at the Swillett.

Until the late 19th century, most water was obtained from artesian wells dug in the grounds of houses, (a typical one still exists at the Manor House, though most others have now been covered). But in 1884, a Rickmansworth Water Works Act was passed, after which the Rickmansworth and Uxbridge Valley Water Co was formed and, by 1885, permission was being sought to extend pipes as far as Harefield.

The water was obtained from bore holes and then pumped into a common system, to which reservoirs were added. At first, it was only necessary to bore down to depths of 15 to 20 feet, but the increase in demand soon caused the water table to drop, with a marked effect on local flora. The pumping station built in 1939 at North Hill, for example, (which incidentally passes for part of its way along the old St Albans-Silchester roadway) has to go down to 300 feet, to the bottom of the valley. Moreover, since this water passes through chalk it was obviously hard, and there was no practical way in which the huge consumption could be softened without incurring enormous expense. Until after Local Government reorganisation, a rate for the water supply was issued separately, but soon after, the water rate was expanded to include the sewage scheme, a matter of singular local injustice, and one which did not pass without comment.

The Gas Light and Coke Company of Rickmansworth was formed in 1852, with total capital assets of £2,084 1s 0d. Shares could be bought for 6d, but by 1869 they had risen in value to £5. Herbert Ingram of Glen Chess was one of its directors, but its mains did not reach Chorleywood till 1907 and, long before then, the Darvell family, with considerable acumen, launched their own gas-making plant, to supply gas for themselves and one or two other interested parties. Later the Watford Corporation bought out the Rickmansworth Company, raising the cost of gas to cover the purchase and, like other public utilities, it was nationalised after the Second World War. Finally, with the finding of huge natural resources, Chorleywood West was converted to natural gas c1971.

The Council also tried to get electricity laid on, the first moves being made about 1908, but it was not until the formation of the Urban District that a contract could be signed between it and the Colne Valley Electricity Company. Then the war intervened, and matters had to remain as they were, the Board of Trade issuing an extension for the Company to honour its agreement after the cessation of hostilities. However, it was not until 3 July 1926, that the Clerk was able to tell the Council that the first cables had been laid and, like other utilities, it was also nationalised after the Second War.

Apart from sewage, the other major concern of the Council was fire hazard, and in 1912 a voluntary brigade was formed, which practised with the hand pump owned and lent by Lady Ela Russell, of Chorleywood House, In 1914 a horse-drawn vehicle with a steam driven pump was purchased by local subscription, and housed in Lower Road, approximately where the public toilets stand now. Horses were borrowed from a Mr Darvell, who ran a taxi service (not the same family as mentioned elsewhere) and, when he decided in the early '20s to change from horses to cars, the problem of traction became acute.

An entry on 25 June 1923 which refers to a fire at Burtons Farm graphically illustrates the problem. The fire was caused by a chicken which knocked over an oil lamp, thereby setting light to some straw. The alarm was sounded at 9.20 pm, and second officer Gathard, together with engineer Dickman, and firemen Sills and Ryder, proceeded to the fire by car, where they joined with the Amersham brigade in working their manual. Fireman Stone, Gathard and Green proceeded to the scene on foot, and driver Craft went to the station, but could not bring the pump into action for lack of horses. Mr Ryman, who was chief of the Brigade, did not hear of the fire till 11.30, when it was well under control, and two hours later, after consultation with Chief Officer Line, the Chorleywood brigade withdrew.

At 10.45 am they received a second call because the fire had broken out again, this time in a straw rick, and this time they arrived in time in good working order, coupling up two horses with jets to work on the blaze. Unfortunately, after half an hour, the water tubes cracked, and the engine ceased to function, so the men turned to help the Amersham brigade, which had arrived in the meantime.

Understandably, the Brigade felt their efforts had been wasted and, in view of the fact that they gave their services voluntarily and unstintingly, they resented the lack of support for the maintenance of equipment. Indeed the Brigade committee offered their resignations and were only prevailed on to withdraw them with some difficulty. The Highways and Commons Committee then set about considering what should be done, and in January 1925 recommended that the Council accept the offer of Messrs Flitt and Co, to convert the existing steamer. The engine and boiler were reconditioned, and the whole mounted on an Albion chassis. By 1951, the pump had outlived its usefulness, and was replaced with a Dennis engine which cost £941 10s 0d.

Fortunately the Brigade was only minimally involved until the Second World War, when the lack of national organisation proved a serious disadvantage, to deal with which the National Fire Service was formed.

Of all these matters, however, it was that of sewage which engaged the most attention, and it was finally decided that, to solve the problem, the Council would have to make its own arrangements, and to do this would have to become a precepting authority in its own right. Accordingly, with Council and Residents' Association backing, Mr Oldham moved, on 8 May 1911, that 'the Parish Council are of the opinion that, owing to the development of the Parish, and the increasing difficulty of dealing with Sanitary and other matters through the agency of the Watford Rural District Council, and the inconvenience of having separate and distinct authorities to deal with various matters, it is expedient to create the whole Parish into an Urban District'.

There were considerable objections from Rickmansworth, who wished to take over Chorley-wood, and include it within their own schemes, with the result that the County arranged for a public enquiry, which took place in 1912. Mr Talbot appeared for Rickmansworth (instructed by Mr Lomas) and Mr J. Schofield (instructed by Mr R. E. H. Fisher) appeared for Chorleywood. Mr Talbot opened the case for Rickmansworth and, after considerable discussion, the Commissioners ruled that the case for Chorleywood should be upheld. On 9 December 1912, a letter was received from the Local Government Board, confirming the County order, and conferring on Chorleywood, Urban District status. The last meeting of the Parish Council took place in the March of the following year.

The formation of the Urban District Authority was closely followed by the murder of the Arch-Duke of Austria, and the opening of hostilities. As a result, on Friday 7 August 1914, the Chairman called an emergency meeting to discuss matters affecting the community; briefly the work in progress, the price of food, and the need for a district fund to alleviate distress.

The Clerk advised the Council that the Government was anxious that the work in hand proceed, and that loan sanctions would be forthcoming. No agreement was reached on food prices, but it was decided to hold a public meeting to consider the formation of a fund raising committee. Shortly after that, a War Relief Committee was established.

On 22 September at another special meeting, Mr Hodges moved the making of a roll of honour of those then serving, and Mr Stacey informed members that 84 had already left to join their regiments. Mr Scott, the surveyor, also asked leave to join, but his services were thought to be indispensable and he was asked to defer his application.

In that November, the Council joined the Urban District Councils Association, and on 4 December they met again to approve model by-laws, which were submitted to the Local Government Board for approval. Then on 26 January 1915, Mr Cotterell was asked to draw up a drainage scheme. The results of his cogitations were modest, costing no more than £1,054 14s 10d, comprising a gravitational system leading to an outlet in the Chess Valley with manhole covers where sewers changed direction, but they had to be shelved for lack of a loan sanction.

Mr Scott was now given leave of absence to join Kitchener's army, the approved by-laws were given the Council's seal, and a discussion followed to consider the shortage of meat. That was in June 1915, and in July the school managers reported that some of their older boys, now nearing the school leaving age of 14, had asked to be given leave early because of the shortage of labour, and the Council agreed to give the five most senior boys permission. At the same meeting the Council also formed itself into a National Registration Committee, on a voluntary basis, to give effect to the requisite Act, and agreed to the Chief Constable's request to restrict lighting on account of the danger from Zeppelins.

In 1916, two councillors were appointed to the local tribunal to deal with conscription. There was a chronic shortage of labour, the fire brigade had the utmost difficulty in continuing, and Mr Jacquet, chairman of the tribunal, resigned following the refusal of his Board to give exemption to the two men whose duty it was to empty the cess pools. No other labourers could be found and the Council had, therefore, to ask that two men engaged in garrison duties take their place.

Despite these problems, the Council nevertheless had time to consider more general matters, and in the same year they even resolved to adopt the decimal system of coinage, and the metric system in general.

By this time the district was fully mobilised for war. Trenches had been dug on the Common, a hut was erected to house members of the bombing school, and a live range had been established on the Common, and to the north of Carpenters Wood Drive. Lady Ela's auxiliary hospital in the grounds of Chorleywood House was functioning, Mr Scott had been promoted to staff sergeant with the RAMC, and Mr Atkins, the Clerk, asked leave to join his colleague; food rationing was introduced. The use of the Common as a live bombing range was totally opposed, without success. This was not only on grounds of a loss of amenity but also on grounds of danger. After the war several nasty accidents occurred from the explosion of dud grenades, which blew up after delayed action. In 1968 the Council was asked to make a search for any remaining bombs, but received no support and it was not until a golfer accidentally uncovered one with a six iron, that a squad of Army engineers undertook a search and found some three hundred dangerous bombs, which had to be exploded on the ground.

On 16 April 1918, the increase of population (resulting from the evacuation of children and the influx of soldiers) had created a dangerous sewage problem but despite a desperate appeal to the Local Government Board, no relief was forthcoming. Six months later the nightmare ended. In all, the district had lost 49 other ranks and three officers, and their names are engraved on a roll of honour in the Memorial Hall, built as a testimonial to those who had fallen.

Slowly the soldiers returned, Mr Atkins resuming his post as Clerk in the March of 1919; Mr Scott, who had received his discharge at the Manchester Infirmary, having spent all his time in Salonika, was given 28 days' leave of absence to see his family, and on 19 July a peace celebration was organised. This followed the usual pattern of a short service at the church, then races and games, and a procession, followed by tea for the children. Each child was given a mug, and Sir Henry Wood provided a conjuror and ventriloquist. For adults, there was wrestling on horseback, dancing and, after a supper given to those who had returned at 7.00 pm, an open air concert and a display of fireworks.

The immediate problems were lack of housing, low wages, and high unemployment. As a result the Government decided to encourage the building of houses for ex-servicemen and working men in general, thus inaugurating a local housing scheme. Offers of land were soon forthcoming and the Council suggested the construction of 58 houses, eight near Sunshine House and 50 at Capel Road. However, the Land Commissioners decided the scheme was too grand, and that it should be revised to 50 houses, ten to an acre.

War savings had played a major role in subsidising the cost of war and, to encourage such savings, local authorities were allotted various field pieces for display. Chorleywood received, in 1920, a German gun carriage which was mounted on the corner of the Common near the hairpin bend by the station, where it remained until removed for salvage in the Second World War.

The other commemorative feature at Chorleywood is the Memorial Hall. A public meeting shortly after the war was held to consider how to commemorate the fallen and it was decided that, for a cost of £5,000, a memorial hall could be built on a site adjoining the Golf Club, which was at that time let to Mr Rose the caterer, who used it to erect a large marquee on festive occasions. At that time, on the land owned by the Golf Club there stood an iron roofed restaurant, which had been the Bothy or canteen for the Loudwater Mill, behind which were some rose arches, and a tea garden, now the putting ground. The Golf Club were not keen on the idea but were short of funds, and the issue was settled by the Council buying the land and letting the Golf Club back to its members, following which the Council used the restaurant for its new District meetings.

It took six months to collect £4,000, but the remainder was slow in coming; nevertheless, by December 1921 the plans for the Hall were complete, in 1922 it was opened, and in 1923 the Council held the first of its meetings there, but this proved unsatisfactory and they then moved back to the Clubhouse until the Second World War.

From the time of its erection the Hall became the centre of many village activities, including the establishment of a lending library. Then, at a branch meeting of the British Legion, Mr Batty gave a gift of £250, and Mr Darvell added another £25, to bring the additional funds already collected up to £1,000, so that a Legion Hall could be added at the back. A foundation stone was laid by Mr Batty in June 1936, and Sir Lionel Halsey presided over the opening on 5 December.

By the '60s the demand for use of the Hall exceeded its possibilities, and another £3,000 was collected for an extension, but this was insufficient and the Council were asked for a grant. In 1968 loan sanction was granted and the building extended over the British Legion Hall at a cost of £11,000, finally completed in 1969. The running of the Hall was conducted by a committee on which the Council were represented, and which for many years was fortunate in having the services of Group Captain Wilson as its supervisor.

Associated with the Hall is, of course, the Royal British Legion, whose Chenies and Chorleywood branch have for so many years supported it so magnificently. Their standard appeared at the Coronation of George VI, and has been seen since at the annual festivals of remembrance in the presence of the Queen. In 1966, when a short summary of their contribution was recorded, they had won the County trophy outright in 1931, 1934, and 1938, and had shared it in 1952, besides providing the County with its standard bearer continuously since 1960. Its main source of income is derived from the sale of poppies and though Mrs Simeons has now died, her work in the district will be long remembered. Less than 10% is used in administration, the rest going in vouchers to the needy and in the upkeep of its homes and industries.

In 1960, it had 200 members, including the County Treasurer, the County Secretary, and the County representative to the Eastern Association. Since then it has grown in strength, and, in truth, the British Legion has never forgotten those who have given their all.

The war over, the burning question of sewage disposal had now to be resolved and, while the Council was prepared to join with Rickmansworth in a scheme, Rickmansworth would consent to nothing short of complete annexation, and the Chairman and Vice-Chairman tendered their resignations on the grounds that the Council had no mandate for amalgamation. Thereafter it was decided to go it alone, and in 1929 a functional scheme was in operation, large enough to serve a population of up 14,000. This was compulsorily bought by the County in 1936.

The next main change arose out of the development of the railways, which reached Rickmansworth in 1874, and Chesham in 1889, following the sale of land to the Metropolitan estates for this purpose by John Gilliat and the Russell family. But the line from Rickmansworth was not electrified until 1962, until when passengers had to alight and change to steam.

Between 1900 and the '20s, a regular coach route existed along the turnpike, which was serviced by the Old Berkeley Coach.

The next major disturbance was the general strike of 1926, when all Council work, manning of trains, matters such as food rationing were carried out by volunteers. Thereafter matters slowly returned to normal, until the Second World War.

Chorleywood had no military targets or guns, though mobile Bofors were brought into action when aircraft were inoperable. The area was designated an interceptor area. It also escaped serious damage, merely losing a few houses, as a result of bomb ditching by bombers in trouble. Only one aircraft was ever brought down, and that was one of our own. It had however, its own Home Guard, and an exceptionally able sergeant who had served in the First World War, Charlie Batchelor, who modelled for Tommy Atkins in that conflict.

However, the generosity of its inhabitants was behond praise; two fully equipped ambulances were given to the district, though fortunately they were never needed locally, one by Miss Dorothy Paget, and another by Mr Swan of the Common and both were later sent to the United Nations Relief and Rehabilitation Association.

During War Weapons Week £104,010, roughly £26 per head of the population, was collected, and subsequently Chorleywood and Rickmansworth bought HMS *Paladin*, at a cost of £61,107, for which the Lords of the Admiralty subsequently presented the District with the ship's crest.

The problems of the Council at this difficult time were not helped by the fact that the Clerk, Mr Blaser, was also the Clerk of Chesham, or by the fact that the Chairman, Capt Higgs was called up. His place was taken by Lady Lorna Lewis who continued to serve throughout the war. Other Council men were also called up, and the work devolved on the united efforts of those that remained with the help of volunteers. Salvage had to be sorted and separated, rationing and National Registration came into force, and had it not been for the devoted service of the Women's Voluntary Service under Lady Lewis, the task might well have proved impossible.

The shortage of food also made it necessary to plough up part of the Common and the Chorleywood House estate, while many gardens were turned into alottments. The children contributed their quota by farming one complete acre.

The Council minutes also mention awards to several local inhabitants. Flying Officer Cadman received the DFC, Major Cadman the MBE, Mr Mergler RN the BEM for mine disposal, Wing Commander Newman a DFC and bar, while the district received a scroll from the Stalingrad bed fund. Fifteen officers and 16 other ranks lost their lives.

The major changes of the post-war period arose from the vast increase in population, which virtually doubled, the building of the North Orbital Road, which caused a furore, and was bitterly opposed, and the re-organisation of local government.

Unfortunately, most of the minutes for Chenies are missing. Chenies never became an urban district, remaining a Parish Council, subordinate to Amersham Rural District Council.

ABOVE: The Gate Inn on the Turnpike, the Gout Road, and BELOW: the
Post Office, Pullens, showing the gas lamps.

ABOVE: The Swan Inn, Rickmansworth, the initial staging post of the second section of the Turnpike road through Chorleywood and Chenies, and BELOW: the Old Berkeley Coach, later the Mills coach, run by Bertram Mills, a superb coachman, who founded the famous Circus.

ABOVE: North Hill, which runs along the course of the Old Verulamium —
Silchester road: the Water Company's pump at the bottom delves 300′ to
reach the water table, once only 15′ beneath the surface; BELOW: Shire
Lane, the County boundary.

LEFT: Quickley Lane, 1936; BELOW: the Herons-gate end of Quickley Lane, 1914, and RIGHT: Old Shire Lane.

LEFT: Whiteland Avenue, once Mainway; RIGHT: the Drive from near the
PNEU School, once the Drive from Rickmansworth to the Cedars;
CENTRE: the Swillet; BELOW: The Coronation Procession, 1911.

LEFT: The underground reservoir of the Rickmansworth and Uxbridge
Valley Water Co, where Roman coins were found; RIGHT: Chenies pump,
and BELOW: Chenies Fire Brigade.

ABOVE: Chorleywood Fire engine and Brigade, and BELOW: Chenies
goes to War, 1914-18.

LEFT: The recreation hut in the Chorleywood Compound, 1914-18; and RIGHT: the auxiliary hospital 1914, CENTRE: Council houses in Solesbridge Close, and BELOW: in Bullsland Gardens.

ABOVE: The Memorial Hall and behind, the Legion Hall; BELOW: Rose's
tea rooms, once the Bothy or Mill Canteen.

LEFT: The Golf Club, used by the Council before moving first to the Memorial Hall and then to Chorleywood House; RIGHT: Chorleywood Station, and BELOW: Charlie Batchelor, the original Tommy Atkins.

ABOVE: Mr Wearing's milk float, in Whitelands Avenue: the milk came from his Hill Farm; CENTRE LEFT: Mrs Holliday's bakery, Lower Road; RIGHT: Gullets' development, Lower Road, showing the banks; BELOW LEFT: the Parade, and RIGHT: the pylons for the North Orbital going up at Berry Lane.

ABOVE LEFT: Panmure Gordon; RIGHT: Parkfield, designed by Lutyens, for another Gordon, a descendant of Alexander Gordon who founded the gin firm. CENTRE LEFT: Sir George and Lady Alexander at RIGHT: Tollgate Cottage; BELOW: the rear view of the Court. (RC).

Behind the Scenes

The colour and character of Chorleywood and Chenies is to be found not only in the pretty village, the lovely Common, or the tree lined avenues, but equally in the biographies of its inhabitants, its numerous societies, and friendly gatherings. On the other hand it is and always has been first and foremost a residential area, where personal privacy is respected. It follows that except on a few public occasions, when its residents open their doors, it is difficult to ferret out its true character. The Loudwater estate, for example, is private and while the public can gain access, they are not encouraged; thus few see the lovely houses, and the river with its water lilies and island.

Much of its beauty is owed to Panmure Gordon, born in 1837, a descendant of Lord Panmure and of the Gordon family, an old Harrovian, loosely connected with Byron and the Marquis of Huntly. When his father went bankrupt this remarkable personality resigned his commission and went to China, joining a firm in Shanghai. There he attracted the attention of General Gordon of Khartoum, who was involved with the suppression of the Tai Ping rebellion, and assumed command of the Shanghai Mounted Ranger Volunteers, when he was decorated for his efforts at the siege of Talv Forts. He loved China, where he made a fortune, and retained many personal mementos of his time there, including a rickshaw and some Sedan chairs.

Returning home he founded the stockbroking firm of Panmure Gordon, which gained such respect that when he died the 'Change closed its doors for the day. He was a great collector, bred a special breed of collies, and gained the friendship of Edward VII and the Kaiser. Among his most treasured possessions was a banner given to his ancestor Glenbucket Gordon, by the Young Pretender, which was left to the National Army Museum. Among his other treasures were a number of exquisite paintings, and letters and memorabilia of Byron, some of the former going to the Royal Scottish Gallery, and the latter to his old School. The Gordon Boys' Home benefitted to the tune of £5,000.

Beyond the estate, a little further along the A404, is the White Horse, the oldest Inn in Chorleywood, said to have belonged, with Dell Farm, to John Johnson, during the time of his feud with the Vicar of Rickmansworth. A little further on, and currently under development is the former estate of Gordon of Gordon's Gin fame, and almost opposite, the bungalow of the late Sir John Wrigley, KBE, CB, who master-minded the evacuation of London during the Second World War.

At the corner of Solesbridge Lane is Pullens, the oldest grocery in Chorleywood, next to which is the working men's club, built for them as a gift by Lady Ela Russell. A little further down, still comemorated by name, is the site of the Forge, where the last blacksmith, Bill Thompson and his wife Beatrice celebrated their diamond wedding, almost opposite the site of the original Methodist Chapel — the Donkey Gate Cathedral, so-called because the old donkeys who used to work for the Mill were buried in the field behind. Robert Turney, who used to live in the little Tudor cottage in the Bottom, remembered that whenever a pig was killed, the occupants of the cottages used to share it. A little further down is the gate to the pasturage of Chorleywood House, whence a public footpath leads to the Fisheries, once a charming cottage embellished with wrought iron leased to the Dulanty's, who kept peacocks.

Almost opposite Pullens is Tollgate Cottage, where Sir George and Lady Alexander lived, while Lutyens supervised the building of The Court, on the corner of Dog Kennel Lane, so named after the Arklow Kennels, where the hounds of the hunt were originally kept. Little can be seen of the Court from outside, but the interior is magnificent, a fitting tribute to the talent of Edwin Lutyens and the theatrical flair of Sir George. Facing the house and hidden from the road are the servants' quarters, built to form a Shakespearean backdrop to the Court, with its centre well-head and openings to stage right and left which lead on to the gardens.

Sir George was born in Reading on 19 June 1858, the son of a Socttish merchant who wished his son to follow him into business. But George was attracted to the stage and, when he finally turned professional, joined W. H. Vernon's repertory company at the Theatre Royal, Nottingham, eventually joining Sir Henry Irving at the Lyceum in the production of *Two Roses*. He stayed with them for eight years, except for a short lapse, before starting his own company at the Avenue Theatre, whence he moved to St James. At that time the French Opera Comique was the rage, but Alexander was determined to put on English productions, taking the risk of producing the first of Oscar Wilde's plays, many of which he presented as actor manager.

He was never a robust man, suffering from diabetes, and eventually dying of tubercolosis, but that did not deter him. He represented St Pancras South on the London County Council from 1907 till 1913, was made a freeman of the Company of Turners in 1908, and was knighted in 1911, becoming the President of the Royal Theatrical Fund, and Vice-President of the Actors' Benevolent Fund.

On the northern aspect of the turnpike, almost opposite, is the Gate Inn; a little further on is the Manor House, which it became when Henly Batty bought the Manor, once Home Farm, a meeting house for Quakers behind which was their burial ground. Next door is the opening to the vault of the Barnes family, and then one sees the entrance to the Flour Milling Research Station, which passed from Belch to the Fitzgerald family, then to the surgeon McNamara, and then the Boultons, who sold it to the present establishment. Fitzgerald was the first paid secretary to the MCC and it was largely due to his efforts that the cricket club came into being. The Club had no pavilion and used a bell tent, which had to be taken down between matches. Funds were collected by holding concerts of the type which would have delighted Miss Joyce Grenfell, who often stayed with her family at Two Gables, the home of Mrs Phipps.

Slightly older is the Golf Club, one of the earliest to be formed on the outskirts of London, laid out at the express request of John Gilliat with the help of the Harrow Masters, who gave it its first cup. In those days the membership read like *Burke's Peerage*. It then had eighteen holes, which have since been reduced to nine, but the games were not without incident. Dress was of course formal—plus fives, a peaked cap and red waistcoat—but the commoners did not like their grazing being upset by golf.

A football club was formed c1890, and in 1911 John Gilliat gave permission for a permanent pavilion, since when a pitch was properly kept. The golf course had to wait until 1922. The pavilion is now shared by both cricket and football clubs, an express condition laid down by the Council in return for an annual grant.

Opposite is the main entrance to the Chorleywood House grounds, just inside which, to the east, is the Lawn Cemetery. Here are held annual fêtes, the Donkey Derby's of the Round Table and so on, a coveted venue with often conflicting dates. To the east one can walk down to the Scouts' compound, or west the Tennis Club, and opposite the old compound was the Schoolroom and the Civil Defence Centre, now taken over by the County as a field study centre. In their heyday under Lady Ela the grounds formed a magnificent park and arboretum, and, when Lady Ela's sister the Flying Duchess had the temerity to pay an aerial visit, she was ordered off in her 'nasty little machine' in no uncertain terms. Lady Ela pulled down the Georgian residence of the Barnes family to make way for the present building, which now belongs to the Council. She was a great benefactress to the district and, though she supported Christchurch, she preferred to take service at St Michaels, the family church, which she usually attended in the company of Dame Madge Kendall, the famous actress who lived near the Cedars.

Beyond the House are the Stables, and then where the original Two Gables stood, are now two homes, one of which bears the original name. It was there that the Barnes family lived before moving to the old Chorleywood House, and they sold it to Wilton Phipps. Granny Phipps became Lord Mayor of Chelsea, and later joined the London County Council, becoming a Dame for her work on the Education Committee. She was clearly a woman of great integrity, and the story that it was in her house that the secret meeting between the Government and Michael O'Connor took place is probably true.

In the Second World War the classics master of Merchant Taylor's School was a member of the Intelligence Service, and he once asked me the difference between French and English dentistry; for a short time one of the great houses in this area had been used by the French resistance and, while there, agents had to have their fillings changed to comply with French modes, but it soon became too small and they moved elsewhere. Secrets of State were no stranger to the district. At the Orchard opposite the Phipp's house was the Sunshine Home for Blind Babies, which was sadly burned down, fortunately with no loss of life. The babies were temporarily accommodated at the Cedars.

The Goat Inn stood on the site of today's vicarage in Chenies, before it moved to become the Bedford Arms. The Chenies cricket ground faced the Post Office and the Baptist Chapel, though the Post Office is no more. The almshouses stood in the grounds of Little Green Street Farm, and the hunt met in the dell opposite the Common. Rose's tea rooms used to be in the iron roofed shed which was the navvies' canteen, where on Sundays when the weather was fine tea was taken on the now putting green. King John's Farm was so named by the Hon Arthur Capell, son of the Earl of Essex, and first Chairman of the Urban District Council; it was once Kings End Farm, since it was there that Rupert's cavalry were routed by musket and cannon fire. Capell was short sighted with pebble spectacles, a shooting cap and cape and never attended a committee meeting, preferring to discuss matters at the open Council, with a sharp wit typical of a QC. His wife went shopping with a goose and when that died, a lamb.

Hall Farm is another Tudor building with beams like iron, as is the Retreat, in the Bottom, opposite the Tudor home of Mrs Holliday, and the restored flint cottages. Round the corner the Old Shepherd was one of the earliest inns, and next door the Shepherds Cottage is also Tudor, with a dell garden which, though small, is a gem in its own right.

In Shire Lane, the boundary between the two Shires, lies the Orchard, one of the first Voysey villas, with its heart shaped openings.

Nearby in Colleyland is the Community Arts Centre, once the Methodist Chapel which replaced the Donkey Gate Cathedral. Just off Orchard Drive is the home of the 2nd Chorleywood Scouts whose only President was Dr Hussey, who sailed with Ernest Shackleton on the *Quest*. The 1st Chorleywood scouts originated at Herbert Parsons' stable in Shire Lane, and are now the Batchworth Sea Scouts. Parsons was a veteran of the Royal Flying Corps who established an oak plantation in Phillipshill.

Sir Henry Wood, the great conductor, lived at Appletree Farm, gave us fireworks on the Common, and strongly supported the Choral Society. 'Timber', as he was affectionately known gave us the Promenade Concerts; perhaps a fitting note upon which to end.

LEFT: The Entrance to the Court, designed by Edwin Lutyens, for Sir George Alexander, (RC) and RIGHT: the Shakespearean backdrop, with artificial well; (RC) CENTRE: Chorleywood Pavilion, and BELOW: Chorleywood Cricket eleven, 1958.

ABOVE LEFT: A long putt on the ninth green; the course is rightly famed for its greens and unusual green bunkers; RIGHT: the Hollybush Club, the Artisans' Clubhouse; CENTRE: the Tennis Club, once the kitchen garden of Chorleywood House; BELOW LEFT: the Stables, Chorleywood House; and RIGHT: Two Gables, one of two houses built on the original site.

LEFT: The Orchard, designed by Voysey, an architectural first; Shire Lane; RIGHT: Chenies cricket ground; BELOW: The Hunt: a view showing the kennels etc from the Dell, the Common, Station Road. OPPOSITE LEFT: The Hunt on the Common; RIGHT: The Hammer; CENTRE: Path from Heronsgate, Chorleywood; BELOW: the village Hall at the Swillet.

THE HOUNDS, CHORLEYWOOD.
OCT. 1907.

ABOVE: Chorleywood Bottom: the listed Tudor Cottage of Mrs Holliday
has no chimney, the fire exhausting through the neighbouring house;
BELOW: the Scout Hut, the second Chorleywood Troop.

ABOVE: President Hussey, presenting his trophy to the troop; Hussey served with Shackleton on his famous Antarctic expeditions; LEFT: Charnswood Cottage, Old Shire Lane; once the game keeper's cottage for Newlands Park; RIGHT: Sir Henry Wood.

Bibliography

Concise English Dictionary of Place Names, The, E. Ekwall, Oxford University Press, 1980.
Historical Antiquities of Hertfordshire, The, Sir H. Chauncey, Mullinger and Holdsworth, 1826.
History of the Blind School for Girls, Phyllis Monk, RNIB.
Latimer, K. Brannigan, John Wright, 1970.
Naval History Branch Reprint, S 4566, 1968.
Roman Roads in Britain, I. D. Margary, John Baker, 1967.
Victoria County History of Bucks Edit W. Page, Dawsons of Pall Mall, 1971.
Victoria County History of Herts Edit W. Page, Dawsons of Pall Mall, 1971.
William Penn the Politician, Joseph Illick, Cornell University Press, 1965.
Original manuscript material is available in County Records Offices in Bucks and Herts, and the Public Records Office, London, and archives of Chorleywood Parish and Urban District Council are now in the possession of Three Rivers Non-Metropolitan Council.

Key to Caption Credits

GC	Godfrey Cornwall
S	Mr Seabright
R& UV Water Co	Rickmansworth and Uxbridge Valley Water Company
HCC	Herts County Council
EVP	Mr E. V. Parrot
MM	McLeod Mathews
RC	Mr Robert Caplin

Index

Subscribers

Presentation Copies

1 Chorleywood Parish Council
2 Chenies Parish Council
3 Three Rivers District Council
4 Chiltern District Council
5 Pullens
6 Chorleywood Bookshop
7 Amersham Library
8 Chesham Library
9 Lady Lorna Lewis

10 George & Jennifer Ray	58 Grelle White	106 Mrs Steel
11 Clive & Carolyn Birch	59 Graham J. Aylett	107 Mrs Boatam
12 Professor Walter Einstein	60 Mrs Round	108 L.H. Welstead
13 P.J.A. Heyden	61 / 63 R. Carley	109 Dr R.H. Fox
14 Mrs K. Avery	64 A. P. Harvey	110 R. Setterfield
15 Mrs J. Parker	65 D.J.Rolfe	111 Mrs I. Sherry
16 / 18 John Guy	66 David Rayvern Allen	112 Mrs P. Eunson
19 Mrs Fox	67 Mr Mash	113 D.M. Findlay
20 Mrs Penn	68 Miss Anne Gibbons	114 E.V. Brummell
21 Juergen H. Ohrt	69 A.J. Wilkinson	115 Mrs P.M. Potter
22 Cicely C. Ryman	70 Mr Simpson	116 Mrs B. Curbishley
23 David Hibbert	71 F.L. Flook	117 / 118 Mrs A.M. Ogden
24 Jill Raby	72 Mrs Goodchild	119 Mrs N. Williams
25 Paul Messenger	73 Mrs Entwistle	120 Mrs C.McL. Morley
26 Miss Jackie Hodgson	74 Mrs Nigel Hardy	121 G. Smith
27 T.J. Hennessy	75 C. & C. Bell	122 Mrs J. Daere
28 Mrs M. Maddock	76 I.S. Turner	123 Mrs R. Meakin
29 N. Russell	77 David Faulkner	124 Mr Joll
30 Mrs E.G. Done	78 Ken German	125 Mrs Salter
31 A.R. Twells	79 Mrs K. Fontava	126 Mrs M. Jackson
32 Kenneth Woolnough	80 Tony Gannt	127 C. Rance
33 / 34 Mr & Mrs J. Oakley-Smith	81 R.D. West	128 Mrs B. Cain
35 Dr Eleanor Clarke	82 J. Moore	129 Norman G. Harrison
36 Peter Chard	83 Mrs Chamberlin	130 Mr Kaplan
37 Frank Thompson	84 Mr & Mrs D.G. Smith	131 Miss R. M. Abbot
38 Mrs L. G. Smith	85 Dennis F. Munn	132 Mrs Ellis
39 Victoria & Albert Museum	86 Mrs M.L. King	133 Arthur L.E. Barron
40 Tessa & John Amess	87 George Coates	134 M. Close
41 Christopher Horne	88 A.M. Schofield	135 Mr Swallow
42 Mrs Joy Fleming	89 Mrs J. Mackenzie	136 Mrs W. Bridgman
43 Mrs D. Clark	90 Miss Jean Taylor	137 Ann Wright
44 Miss Sylvia Brown	91 John Decker	138 Mrs Carol Holland
45 Mrs E. Van Schaik	92 Mrs M. Everett	139 John Moss
46 Miss J. Bailey	93 S.W. Hillier	140 Mrs Tibbles
47 Mrs G. Gibbins	94 Mrs G.A. Craven	141 Mrs G.R. Timmons
48 S.R. Butchers	95 R.J. Underwood	142 Miss Wallington
49 Jill Leeming	96 Mrs P.R. Dickins	143 Mrs B.A. Collins
50 Elizabeth Gull	97 Mrs J. Roitt	144 Mrs Rolfe
51 Mrs Whitfield	98 Suzanne McKellar	145 D.W. Pratt
52 Elizabeth Ogan	99 Rae Evans	146 Mr & Mrs M. Reynolds
53 Colin Parkes	100 K. E. Owens	147 Mrs MacNeill
54 D. Bound	101 M. Soper	148 L. Beeson
55 Miss M. R. Bloomfield	102 Mrs C. Forte	149 Beryl Landen
56 Miss H. Spooner	103 Mrs J. King	150 The Rt Rev David Pytches
57 Mrs Holnquist	104 Mrs P. Denby	151 G. Thorogood
	105 Mr Maskell	152 Mrs Marsh

153 Bryan Pratt
154 Mrs Taylor
155 Miss Baker
156 Mrs De Waay
157 G.J. Bastin
158 Mr Hubbard
159 Mrs P. Lingwood
160 S. Whitworth
161 Jean Stell
162 K. Green
163 John A. Gloag
164 Mrs D. Smith
165 Delphia Garger
166 Mrs Clarke
167 J. Marriott
168 Mr Barlow
169 Mrs V. Skinner
170 Miss Joyce A. Mason
171 Mrs S. Gradidge
172 Mrs E.M. Hanison
173 Keith Clark
174 D. Malone
175 Miss R. Spencer
176 F.T. Horne
177 A.E. Ford
178 Ms H.C. Ali
179 Mr & Mrs Hart
180 P.G.H. Evans
181 Mrs Cook
182 J.E. Wright
183
185 Mr Cohen
186 Miss J. Fraser
187 R.D. Wedgerfield
188 Mrs N. Howe
189 Miss B.M. Ruston
190 Mr Groves
191 Teresa Zana
192 M.J. Snowden
193 R.H. Leach
194 M.J. Bubb
195 E.A. Life
196 Mrs M. Foster
197 Mrs P. Hubble
198 Mr & Mrs L.C. Gaskell
199 Mrs Haynes
200 Mrs Shipway
201 Gene & Laurel Emrick
202 Paul & Joan Robertson
203 Mrs Hopkins
204 Mrs Fogden
205 Mrs Mead
206 B. Boden
207 Mr Gowshall
208 Norma Weetes
209 Mrs P.D. Baker
210 Mrs Bilbo
211 Mrs S.R. Watling
212 Mr & Mrs J. McNally
213 Mrs R. Meakin

214 J. Haynes
215 D. Thorpe
216 Alexandra Fowkes
217 B. Fawssett
218 Mr & Mrs Page
219 Mr & Mrs E.W. Lewis
220 P.F. Fonstad
221 H.S. Lee
222 Mrs B.A. Stainton
223 Isabel Daw
224 Norma Tranghar
225 R.M.M.B. Sharp
226 P. Hood
227 Mr & Mrs Kenneth Palmer
228 Dr H.M. Cockle
229 Iris Pashley
230 Mr & Mrs C. Foxell
231 Dr & Mrs C. Foxell
231 Dr & Mrs J. Robinson
232 Anthony Moss
233 T. Trafford Boughton
234 Mrs C.A. Bates
235 Gene Emrick
236 Shirley & Tony Hayzelden
237 Philip Flamank
238
239 E.R. Boxall
240 Gwen Blurton
241 P.G. Hart
242 Robert Caplin
243 Sarah Butler
244 C.E. Keysell
245 C.J. Seabright
246 E.J. Wright
247 D.A. Longman
248 Peter Harmon
249 Ruth Elaine Marshall
250 Jonathan Swift
251
252 Martin Wrigley
253 Chorleywood Field Studies
     Centre
254
255 Trafford Boughton
256 G.P. Ridout
257 R.A.L. Trotman
258 Mrs A.D. White
259 P. McDowell
260 A.R.E. Northcott
261 Mrs R.M. Quail
262 J.A. Bey
263 G.F. Furze
264 D.R. Walker
265 Julia Edwards
266 L.E. & E. Tregoming
267 Margot Willsher
268 Christopher John Reid
269 N. Didwell
270 A.J. Ireland
271 Leonard J.B. Spencer

272 Mrs Kathy Wroath
273 G.W. Creighton
274 Mrs I.W. Pashley
275 Dr Challoners High School,
     Amersham
276 F.T. Horne
277 Lord Paget of Northampton
278 Halen Neve
279 Mrs Jill Riley
280 Nini Stringer
281 E.A. Stranks
282 D.E. Mitchell
283 R. Carpenter
284 Audrey Wright
285 Mrs M. Carter
286 D. Lloyd-Rees
287 Mrs Wendy Dodd
288 Mrs A.S. Davies
289 Caroline Emma Surey
290 Mrs P.M. Shurlock
291 Mrs B. Savin
292 C.F. Stoke
293 M.H. Perry
294 J. Lowe
295 G. Gardner
296 Phyllis Dudley
297 Bailey
298 E.J. Adams
299 Mrs Stewart
300 Mrs M.R. Corfield
301 Margaret Stoneley
302 R.C. Galer
303 B.S.T. Durling
304 Miss E. Barry
305 Mrs A. Lovegrove
306 Professor Askew
307 G.I.C. Thomson
308 Dr P.G. & E.W.W. Owston
309 Joyce Ward
310 R.U. West
311 Martin McLellan
312 Gerald Punton
313 T.M. Shaddock
314 Mrs Audrey
315 A.W. Burton
316 Mrs S.P. Berriman
317 Lionel William Humphrey
318
319 G. & M. Perkins
320 B. Mawhinney
321 Walter James &
     Mary Parry Irving
322 Miss Patsy Hood
323
338 Hertfordshire County Library
339 Charles Bray
340 Buckinghamshire
     County Library

Remaining names unlisted:

ENDPAPERS — FRONT: The 1805 map of Charleywood given by the
Barnes family to Chorleywood Urban District Council; BACK: the 1882/3
OS 25″ map of Chorleywood and Chenies.

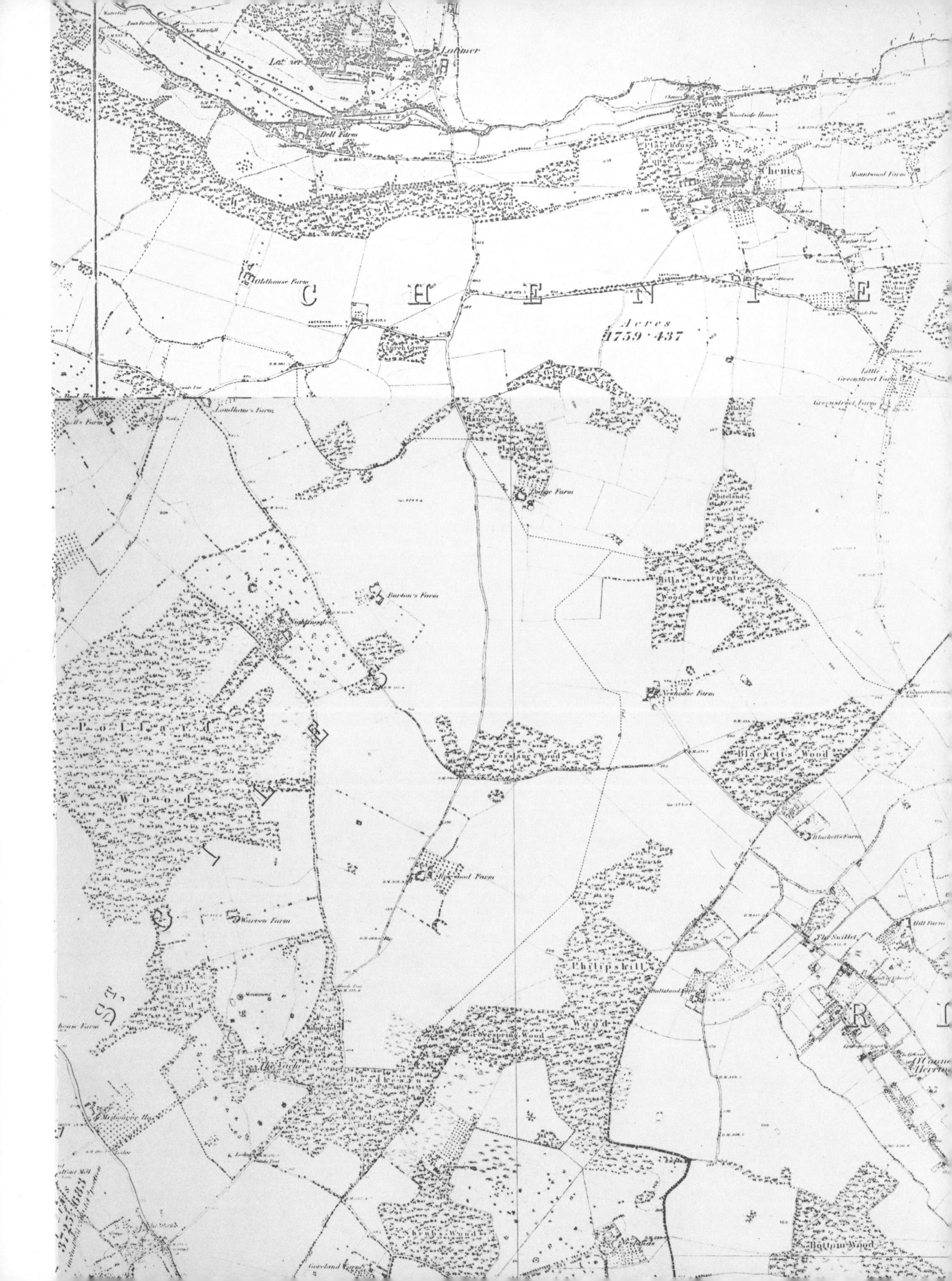

Latimer
Latimer
Dell Farm
Chenies
Woodside House
Mountwood Farm
Little Greenstreet Farm
Greenstreet Farm
Oldhouse Farm
C H E N I E S
Acres
1759·437
Church Grove
Loudham's Farm
Hanging Wood
Lodge Copse
Lodge Farm
Whiteland's
Burton's Farm
Nightingale
Millar Carpenter's Wood
Newhouse Farm
Carpenter's Bottom
Pollards
Blackett's Wood
Wood
Blackett's Farm
Gorelane Wood
Warren Farm
Raymond Farm
Hill Farm
The Swillet
Monument
Philipskill
Hallaland Farm
Grovespring Wood
Wood
R
Herring
Mulberry Ho.
The Vache
Brush Wood
Bottom Wood
Flint Mill
Gorelane Cottages